Somatic
Intelligence
for Success

Nervous System Alignment
to Prevent Burnout and
Leave an Impact

Sheridan Ruth

SOMATIC INTELLIGENCE FOR SUCCESS:

NERVOUS SYSTEM ALIGNMENT TO PREVENT BURNOUT AND LEAVE AN IMPACT

SHERIDAN, RUTH

For more information: hello@sheridanruth.com

ISBN PAPERBACK: 978-1-962280-82-2
ISBN EBOOK: 978-1-962280-83-9

This is a book for every entrepreneur, leader, founder, and professional who has ever felt in their heart that there is a better way to operate in the world—where health, equality, peace, and freedom feature in the heart of each individual—but feels overwhelmed and exhausted trying to pursue their success and purpose without sacrificing themselves.

Table of Contents

Introduction

There's something I know about you. It's something that you and I have in common, and sometimes it might even feel like a bit of a secret. Deep down, once we get past that loud inner critic and our acute sense of inadequacy, we both know there's something inside of us—something that, if everyone else could see it, or if even we could see it fully and more consistently, would change the world. You have a solution, a way of being, or a perspective that others need, and you've been working hard to get it to the people who need it most.

We knew it would be hard, and it's not that we shy away from hard work, but sometimes it feels like there's this invisible wall between fulfilling our purpose with ease and the reality of where we are today. And if I think I know you—and I think I do—you've probably tried perfectly organizing your time. You've been to therapy, you've tried positive thinking, and you've pushed harder, maybe even to the point of burnout after weeks of overworking.

Yet, like me, you sometimes find yourself waking up at four in the morning, worried about your messaging or your clients, or running spreadsheets about money in your head. You may find yourself neglecting your health and relationships in the process. And while this journey can be hard, it's also deeply fulfilling, and deep down, you wouldn't change it for anything in the world. But you also know that you've got to figure out a way to make it a lot easier on yourself.

That's why you're here.

I wrote this book to help you build an impactful, purposeful business without compromising your mental or physical health or your values. It's the formula that helped me do it once and helps me maintain my success, health, and ease even when I'm in massive life changes, crippled with self-doubt, tired, or just about to get my period and experiencing every emotion known to (wo)man in a span of twenty-four hours.

There's something that we will need to agree on before we go much further, and it's the following: building an impactful, purposeful business without compromising your mental or physical health, or your values, will not come from following someone else's path to their success, especially if you want an extraordinary life with extraordinary success. Meaning you want it all—wealth, health, positive cultural change, healthy relationships, and a sense of fulfillment—and you deserve it. You truly do.

However, extraordinary success isn't achieved through mainstream and ordinary approaches to entrepreneurship. It's achieved through nontraditional, extraordinary approaches (which are hidden in your body). This book will show you how to find your extraordinary path to success.

It's created for *you*. Whether you're cultivating your first $5,000 months or leading your established company into new ventures, we will use the Body Based Business® (BBB) methodology to take you from overthinking, being exhausted, and feeling stuck to feeling on track, energized, and excited by how your business creates change in the world (without compromising your mental or physical health or your values).

You'll also learn how to do the following:

- Overcome the most commonly misunderstood aspects of listening to your body, regulating your nervous system, and creating success on your own terms.
- Access self-compassion by understanding that the basic science of your nervous system has been making your path so far much harder than it ever needed to be.
- Create a strategy that works with your nervous system and helps you achieve each and every one of your goals in record time with minimal effort.
- Learn how to increase your income *and* see your purpose out in the world.

One of the most enjoyable and effective aspects of this book is that you'll be able to learn all of this with ease because you'll be learning through a story. Our brains retain information through stories more than they do through other methods of presenting information. You'll be learning through two characters, Debbie and Emily, as they go through the business performance program, Body-Based Business®, and learn how to build sustainable, profitable, and purposeful businesses using the wisdom of their nervous systems. Debbie and Emily have been carefully curated from a combination of common client cases I've worked on and personal experience.

Who am I and why am I qualified to support you?

As you read my story, you might feel inspired, thinking, *If it was possible for her, then it's possible for me.* On the other hand, you might compare my story to your own and notice some pretty big differences between us. Thoughts might cross your mind like *She hasn't experienced what I have—she doesn't know how to help* or even *She's not that impressive.* In both cases, you may be running into a pattern that actually keeps you from creating lasting, sustainable change in your life.

In the first scenario—using my story as proof that you can achieve your goals—you might be engaging in reassurance seeking. Reassurance seeking provides temporary relief and a boost in confidence, which feels amazing. But research shows it can actually increase anxiety over time.[1] Why? Because when we look to others (books, studies, social media influencers, or even friends) for assurance, the effect doesn't last; it's not rooted in your personal experience. Your mind latches onto hypothetical ideas of what could apply to you based on others' experiences, but this will never fully satisfy your body's need for certainty and confidence in what genuinely fits your life right now.

In this book, you'll learn to cultivate such strong self-belief and self-trust that you'll be able to build your business on your terms, achieving both physical health and financial empowerment. You won't rely as heavily on inspiring stories; instead, you'll gain insights and education from a broad range of sources, enhancing your ability to effectively achieve your goals.

The path to truly believing in yourself and knowing that your dreams are possible lies in gathering information from sources (like this book) and then experimenting with how it applies to you in the real world. There's no rush—this process is embedded in the BBB methodology. You'll be given the tools and support to build confidence in your inner voice, your vision, and your dreams. I've got you.

---

1. Neil A. Rector, Katy Kamkar, Stephanie E. Cassin, Lindsay E. Ayearst, and Judith M. Laposa, "Assessing excessive reassurance seeking in the anxiety disorders," *Journal of Anxiety Disorders 25*, no. 7 (2011): 911–917, https://doi.org/10.1016/j.janxdis.2011.05.003; Van Bui and David A. Moscovitch, "Predictors of Excessive Reassurance Seeking in Social Anxiety," *Cognitive Therapy and Research 48*, no. 2 (2024): 292–302, https://doi.org/10.1007/s10608-024-10473-1.

Now, if you tend to compare my story to yours and focus on the differences, recognize that these thoughts likely stem from a primal, protective mechanism built within us that prefers to keep things exactly as they are. Your body and brain are designed to preserve energy and keep you safe. No matter how much your heart and mind may want to change, the fact that you're reading this now means you're alive, and your body is doing its job. It may also sense that making changes will require some upfront energy and effort, though in the long term, you'll save energy, improve your health, and thrive. But right now, your body can't see that.

Take a moment to step outside your thoughts. Can you observe them without fully believing them? Could you approach this process with an open mind about what you might learn? Because if you choose to find value here, you will—and you'll walk away with a taste of sustainable success you never thought was possible. Don't worry; you'll be guided through how to do this from many different perspectives as we dive into the content.

When I was seven years old, I lost all my hair due to an incurable autoimmune disease (alopecia universalis), which left a mark on my self-esteem that would follow me into a very dark chapter of my life. I found myself in a physically, emotionally, financially, and sexually abusive relationship, which I ended through the courageous decision to leave. At that time, I was isolated in a foreign country, far from home and community, and shortly after, my ex chose to end his life. In the months following his suicide, events unfolded that I still struggle to believe could have happened. The world around me unraveled, and I encountered the darkest sides of people I had known.

Up until that moment, I'd been studying community development and spending most of my time in small entrepreneurial ventures and volunteering with local charities. These events hit just as I officially graduated and entered the workforce, but I was a shell of a human being. Diagnosed with complex PTSD and caught in emotional ups and downs that left me barely able to function, I found my life dark and confusing. My low self-esteem, lack of self-trust, anxiety, and depression led me to decisions that only deepened the downward spiral I couldn't seem to escape—until two pivotal moments changed everything.

The pivotal moment that set everything in motion came after a particularly tough therapy session and a transformative yoga class. Traditional healing methods weren't helping, but during yoga, as I twisted, stretched, and relaxed into pose after pose, I felt a small release in my heart each time. It was beautiful but not enough, and I sensed, deep in my gut, that something better was out there. My fingers found their way to my laptop, and a quick search led me to somatic (body-based) trauma therapies.

With these tools, my own somatic intelligence, and the guidance of some amazing mentors, coaches, and training, I was finally able to function in the world again and started building a yoga therapy business. If we had met back then, you might have said I was strong, interesting, and inspiring. On paper, I looked like I had recovered: I was feeling empowered about my hair loss (wearing a wig less often), had founded a popular nonprofit organization, was teaching wellness to the United Nations, and was closing million-dollar real estate deals. But beneath it all, there was still an ache, a quiet turmoil lingering inside.

The next breakthrough that pushed me forward came when the world collapsed into quarantine in 2020. I was forced to take my small business online, and the cracks in my psyche became glaringly obvious.

Entrepreneurship was exhausting me. Other coaches seemed to know what they were doing, and I felt completely lost. Each time I opened my laptop, I saw other coaches' wins and celebrations, then I'd switch to a blank Google doc and stare at the cursor blinking back at me. I felt paralyzed by the fear of rejection when writing content; my voice would shake as I searched for the perfect way to express the value of my offer. And if I did manage to book a sales call, a heaviness would settle in my chest, and my mind would fog over as I listened to potential clients speak.

In surrender, I mentally quit entrepreneurship and tried to will myself to start applying for jobs. But my body felt as heavy as lead, so I used a breathing practice I'd learned from somatic trauma therapy training just to find the strength to turn off the taps and step over the shower threshold.

With my spine a little straighter, a thought surfaced: *What if I could use this intelligence in my business? What if that was the key—not someone else's templates, proven pathways, or structures, but that small, guiding voice inside me?*

I began taking action from this intelligence, learning to access it more deeply and to build a business and lifestyle that both protected and supported it. From that point on, even though I was still healing from past pain and navigating a chaotic world, I created a wonderfully profitable business that filled me with a fulfillment and purpose unlike anything I'd ever experienced. It moves me to tears as I write this. This methodology and business have been the greatest gift I've given myself, the people around me, and the world.

Others started noticing the radiance I brought to my work and saw that I had accomplished something many strive tirelessly for. I had achieved something they had been dreaming of, and they wanted help doing the same. So, I began helping. Ten people turned into a hundred, and the numbers kept multiplying. That's when the BBB methodology, which you're about to learn, was born. It's been tried and tested on myself and countless others across many industries, and now, it's ready for you.

Key Foundations of The Body Based Business Methodology

This book is grounded in the understanding that our biology shapes how we think, live, interact, work, and perceive the world. It also asserts that each person carries an inner intelligence aligned with the laws of nature—an intelligence that, when unlocked, leads us toward a life of abundance and harmony. This intelligence doesn't promise a life free of challenges, but it does provide a pathway to finding our unique place in the world, one where we feel fully alive, with purpose, abundance, peace, and joy. It guides us on how to engage with the tangible aspects of the world, including our work, money, and vision.

You don't have to believe this yet. In fact, your skepticism is welcome. As you go through this book, think of these beliefs as something to try on, like a jacket. See how they fit in *your* life (not your friend's or your mother's, but yours). Approach it like a scientist, experimenting to see what you discover as you apply these methods.

Your experiment will unfold in phases:

1. We'll start with foundational understanding and tips on getting the most from this book.
2. Next, we'll explore how to tap into your body's wisdom to reach your goals.

3. With this foundation of safety and body intelligence, you'll learn to unburden yourself from the toughest parts of your entrepreneurial journey.

4. Then, with a sense of clarity and energy, you'll be ready to think creatively about how to apply this to your larger business strategy, marketing, sales, and leadership, from your big vision down to daily tasks.

5. Finally, you change the world in two ways. First is the ripple effect; you'll become someone who, by going about their day with joy, ease, and peace, creates a strong ripple effect that makes the world a more enjoyable, peaceful place to live. Secondly, because you're no longer putting so much energy into fixing yourself, understanding yourself, and avoiding, repressing, or healing your pain, you get to put your energy into bigger problems in the world and solve them—effectively and without sacrificing yourself.

Ultimately, the world becomes a better place because you found your ease, success, and resilience—and I'm not exaggerating.

Let's get into it!

Foundations of Body Based Business

Chapter 1

Where Your Nervous System and Your Vision Collide

It was day one of the Body Based Business Academy, and Debbie and Emily were sitting in cold, rigid chairs, notebooks open in front of them, backpacks by their sides—prepared but feeling desperately alone. They each looked around the room, sizing everyone up, noticing bags and clothes, and imagining stories about who each person was. Both glanced down at their intake forms, unaware that they had written nearly identical phrases like "It feels like everyone has something figured out that I don't," and "I'd be embarrassed if people knew I actually felt this way." Had they been able to look at everyone else's paper, they would've seen that each person felt almost exactly the same way, regardless of their profession, goals, or backgrounds.

That day, I learned a little more about Debbie. She was a fiery, passionate brand consultant who had recently left her full-time job to pursue her calling—empowering social enterprises by helping them communicate their mission effectively. She had watched so many visionaries and creatives get bogged down in vague, fluffy language that wasn't helping them reach their goals. Debbie believed wholeheartedly in the power of branding and storytelling to reach people's hearts and drive real change.

Yet, every morning, she woke with anxiety in her chest and a racing heart, afraid of the risks of entrepreneurship, terrified of going broke, and overwhelmed by the endless mountain of tasks on her to-do list. Her insecurities, along with her IBS (irritable bowel syndrome), threatened to make the journey even harder. She couldn't fully pinpoint what was wrong, but she knew something wasn't right. Each new client took a toll on her energy, and she was beginning to question whether her dream would ever work out.

Emily, too, shared that feeling of being held back, despite a burning desire to do something meaningful and impactful in the world. She wanted to contribute, to leave a legacy. She had a beautiful concept for a digital mental health product and offered wellness consulting to larger corporations. Although she had her design team in place and experience to draw on, and despite everyone around her telling her she was capable, she wrestled with deep-seated feelings of inadequacy. She doubted herself, thinking she didn't know enough, wasn't smart enough, couldn't actually succeed. She believed her achievements up to this point had been mere flukes and just couldn't see what others saw in her. Mornings felt heavy, and she often struggled to get out of bed. It was this strange mix of physical lethargy and mental fog that made everything feel like an insurmountable task. Every decision sent her spiraling into overthinking, and this constant mental tug-of-war left her anxious and drained.

What neither Debbie nor Emily understood was that their nervous systems were in a state of dysregulation. Their bodies perceived their ambitious business goals as a threat to their safety, preventing them from accessing the clarity, emotional balance, and inspired action they needed to thrive. This dysregulation was the hidden reason they felt scattered, exhausted, and like their efforts weren't yielding the results they'd hoped for.

To overcome this, the first step was understanding the role of the nervous system in entrepreneurship. With awareness and education, Debbie and Emily could start creating sustainable change, building the impactful, purpose-driven businesses they had envisioned. Here's what the first session covered—and how you can begin applying it to your own life.

How the Nervous System Is Affecting Your Success

In this chapter, I'll be using terms like *neuroception, ventral vagal, sympathetic,* and *dorsal vagal* to explain certain concepts. But remember, your success with this book isn't measured by how well you remember these words. Honestly, it took me a couple of years to feel confident that I was using them correctly every time, and I teach this nearly every day. If you feel naturally drawn to learn these terms, follow that! If not, feel free to set them aside and focus instead on the corresponding colors or the "felt sense" of each state in your body. This approach has worked well for both me and my clients. What matters most is that you begin to understand how your own nervous system works and how your body communicates with you.

Your body communicates through one central system that absorbs information from your environment and coordinates with every other system in your body—from digestion to hormones to sleep cycles. This is the foundation of your autonomic nervous system or ANS.

The ANS is a complex network of nerves and cells that has evolved over millennia and is remarkably consistent in its design across all humans. It's called *autonomic* because it operates on autopilot. It regulates (meaning it controls and directs according to its own rules, structures, and processes) essential functions like heartbeat, breathing rhythms, blood pressure, digestion, and metabolism. Its biggest job, however, is to manage energy—storing, conserving, and releasing it based on internal and external cues, in whatever way it perceives will best support your safe movement through the day. It operates on something like a programmed setting that influences how you perceive the world, the thoughts and emotions you experience, and the actions you take.

The way your ANS regulates (by moving energy and generating thoughts, emotions, and sensations) shapes your entire experience with entrepreneurship and leadership. When it senses danger, you'll encounter physical, mental, and emotional challenges in various forms. This might show up as a constant feeling of being on edge, difficulty focusing, or even feeling physically drained. However, because this system can be understood and adjusted, you can learn to navigate the ups and downs of entrepreneurship with greater ease, creativity, resilience, and flow. This not only makes the journey more sustainable but also helps you become even more effective in your work.

Breaking Down the Autonomic Nervous System

According to polyvagal theory, the ANS has two branches—the sympathetic and parasympathetic—and operates in three different states, all governed by the vagus nerve.

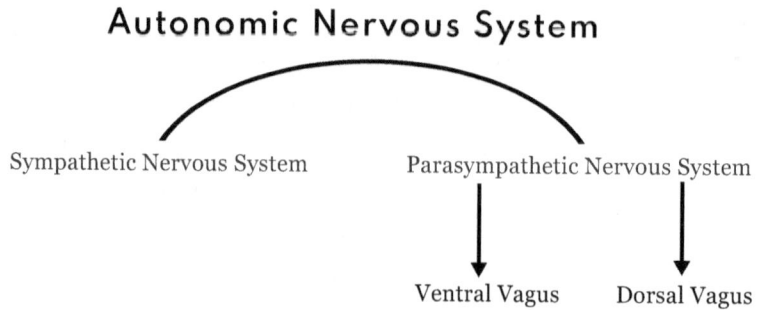

The vagus nerve is a bundle of nerves that run from your brain stem through your neck and down to major organs like the heart, lungs, and digestive system. The vagus nerve helps regulate these autonomic responses, switching between sympathetic (fight or flight), dorsal vagal (shut down), and ventral vagal (regulated and connected) states as your body responds to internal and external cues. It's the vagus nerve's activation of these branches and states that influences your overall sense of safety, calm, or stress.

When your nervous system perceives a threat, it may become dysregulated, moving into either the sympathetic or dorsal vagal states as a way to protect you. Here's how each branch and state functions:

States in the parasympathetic branch

The **parasympathetic** branch helps the body conserve energy, lowers your heart rate, and facilitates energy to your digestive organs so that you can digest; when you are in a stressed state, the body is not worried about digesting food—it's worried about running from a tiger!

When you feel safe and calm, your nervous system is in the **ventral vagal state**, which is part of the parasympathetic branch. This state supports social engagement, relaxation, and healthy digestion. You can connect easily with others, feel at ease, and approach the day with a sense of security and well-being. This is where you'll feel grounded, creative, and able to focus on yourself and the world around you. You may feel this ventral vagal response as you read these words. I will later refer to this state as the *green zone*.

If stress becomes overwhelming or inescapable, your nervous system may shift to the **dorsal vagal state**, another part of the parasympathetic branch.

This state is the body's way of conserving energy when it feels powerless or unable to escape. Often associated with feelings of helplessness, depression, or disconnection, it can lead to numbness, confusion, and withdrawal. In the dorsal vagal state, your body slows down digestion and reproductive energy, meaning you may experience digestive issues or a lack of sexual and creative drive. The body is focused on survival by conserving energy, rather than on connecting or creating. You may feel this dorsal vagal response as you read these words. I will later refer to this state as the *blue zone*.

States in the sympathetic branch

The sympathetic branch is responsible for increasing heart rate, releasing adrenaline, dilating pupils, and redirecting blood flow to muscles in preparation for quick action.

When you encounter stress—like a difficult client demanding a refund—your nervous system may shift into the **sympathetic state**. Known as the "fight-or-flight" response, this state prepares your body for immediate action by increasing your heart rate, tensing muscles, and redirecting energy away from functions like digestion. The sympathetic state is all about survival: mobilizing energy to confront or escape from danger. You may feel more alert and ready to act, but staying here for too long can lead to burnout and exhaustion. I will later refer to this state as the *red zone* or the *yellow zone* (depending on if we are referencing fight or flight respectively).

We will return to an understanding of these states, or zones, in different ways throughout the book; however, the most important part to remember at this point is the difference between regulation (ventral vagal) and dysregulation (sympathetic and dorsal vagal), as well as the impact of extended time spent in dysregulated states, which is what we'll cover next.

The Impact of Your Nervous System on Entrepreneurship

Time spent in dysregulated states can include the following:

- Chronic anxiety and worry
  - o Persistent feelings of fear, tension, and unease, especially around decision-making, can indicate that the nervous system is stuck in a heightened state of alert. This makes it difficult to take risks, think creatively, or stay focused.
- Procrastination and avoidance
  - o Overwhelm can lead to procrastination, especially on tasks that feel too big or too uncertain. This is a form of a freeze response in which the nervous system shuts down in an attempt to protect you from perceived threats.
- Difficulty focusing
  - o When the body thinks it's unsafe, it will remain alert to its surroundings, and you may struggle to concentrate, leading to scattered thinking, inability to prioritize, and difficulty completing tasks efficiently (basically, you're overwhelmed and unproductive).
- Physical symptoms
  - o A dysregulated nervous system triggers an overactive stress response, keeping the body in a prolonged state of fight, flight, or freeze, which leads to physical symptoms like headaches, muscle tension, digestive issues such as IBS, and chronic fatigue due to the body's inability to properly restore balance and recovery.
- Emotional instability
  - o Mood swings, irritability, or feeling easily overwhelmed by small challenges can indicate that the nervous system is not

regulating emotions effectively, which is both due to, and creating, dysregulation. We'll go into more detail around emotions in chapter 9.

- Hypervigilance
  - Constantly feeling on edge, like you're waiting for the next crisis, can be a sign of nervous system dysregulation and lead to chronic exhaustion.
- Difficulty making decisions
  - When the nervous system is dysregulated, decision-making becomes challenging because your body is putting its energy into protecting itself from danger.
- Isolation or disconnection
  - Feeling disconnected from others or withdrawing socially can be a sign that the nervous system is in a survival mode and believes it needs to protect itself from others.
- Stifled creativity and innovation
  - A dysregulated nervous system is conserving energy to protect itself and will therefore limit the capacity you have to think creatively and come up with innovative solutions, which are critical for growing your business and income.
- Increased risk aversion
  - When the nervous system is in a constant state of dysregulation, it will miscalculate risks and believe average risks are more dangerous than they really are. This fear of failure or making mistakes can prevent you from seizing opportunities.
- Burnout leading to decreased capacity
  - A dysregulated nervous system is prone to overworking and is unable to find deep rest. This means it's likely

to experience burnout, reducing your overall capacity to work effectively. This can result in missed income opportunities, less client interaction, and decreased overall business growth.

- Negative money mindset
  - o A sense of insecurity in the body due to a dysregulated nervous system can create and reinforce disempowering beliefs about money, which affects how you approach pricing, sales, and financial decisions. In chapter 11 we'll look into how this can limit your income potential.
- Difficult client relationships
  - o Nervous system dysregulation gives the body the sense that it is unsafe to connect with other humans which can lead to potential conflicts, misunderstandings, or loss of business.
- Reduced confidence in value
  - o A dysregulated nervous system can create and reinforce disempowering beliefs around your worth and the value of your services, leading to underpricing or a reluctance to market yourself, which directly affects your income.
- Missed opportunities
  - o When your nervous system is dysregulated because your mind is prioritizing keeping you alive and maintaining you in the known (and what it believes to be secure), you're more likely to overlook or pass on opportunities that could increase your income, whether it's networking, collaborations, or investments, due to your inability to manage the additional stress.

Entrepreneurship with a Regulated Nervous System

When you regulate your nervous system approach, your entrepreneurship journey will be hallmarked by the following characteristics:

- Calm confidence and clarity
  - Instead of chronic anxiety and worry, you'll feel a steady sense of calm and self-assurance. Decision-making becomes smoother, risks feel more manageable, and you'll trust your instincts and creative abilities to guide you toward success.
- Purposeful action and momentum
  - Procrastination and avoidance transform into decisive action. You'll be able to achieve your tasks and end each day feeling a sense of accomplishment.
- Focused flow and productivity
  - With a well-regulated nervous system, focus becomes second nature. You'll prioritize with ease, maintain a steady workflow, and complete tasks with efficiency, making space for even more creativity and innovation.
- Vibrant physical health and vitality
  - Physical symptoms like headaches and muscle tension will significantly decrease, and you'll experience more vitality and energy. You'll feel physically aligned with your work, ready to meet the challenges of the day with resilience and strength.
- Emotional balance and resilience
  - Emotional instability shifts into a balanced, grounded emotional state. You'll handle challenges with grace, remaining composed even under pressure, which leads to better decisions and outcomes for your business.

- Relaxed presence and trust
  - o Hypervigilance turns into a state of calm awareness. You'll see everything is unfolding as it should. You'll no longer be constantly on edge, which allows you to relax, recharge, and stay productive without burnout.
- Confident and decisive leadership
  - o Instead of struggling with decision-making, you'll approach choices with confidence and trust in your own judgment. You'll be able to put aside second-guessing and navigate uncertainty with ease and clarity.
- Connected and supportive relationships
  - o Meaningful connection will help you easily engage with your community, build strong relationships, and draw inspiration from your interactions, knowing that you have a supportive network to lean on.
- Increased income and abundance
  - o Productivity skyrockets when your nervous system is regulated, leading to better organization and efficiency. You'll complete projects on time, meet deadlines, and seize new opportunities that boost your income potential.
- Unleashed creativity and innovation
  - o A calm nervous system fuels creativity. You'll tap into innovative solutions and new ideas with ease, allowing your business to thrive and evolve, leading to sustained growth and increased financial rewards.
- Bold risk-taking for growth
  - o Rather than avoiding risks, you'll embrace them with calculated confidence. You'll recognize opportunities for significant financial gain and feel empowered to act on them, propelling your business forward.

- Resilience and sustainable capacity
  - Instead of burnout, you'll feel energized and capable of maintaining your business at a high level. With sustainable practices, you'll increase your capacity for growth without sacrificing your well-being.
- Empowered money mindset
  - You'll have the space to find more empowering beliefs about money and truly feel a sense of security and abundance. You'll approach pricing, sales, and financial decisions with confidence, knowing your worth and charging appropriately for your services or product.
- Positive client relationships
  - Your body's propensity to connect to others, instead of protecting itself, will help you create strong, trusting, and productive relationships with clients. This ensures smoother collaborations, repeat business, and referrals, boosting your revenue and reputation.
- Confidence in your value and offerings
  - A regulated nervous system gives you the embodied sense of confidence to no longer doubt yourself or your offerings. You'll confidently market yourself and charge your worth, knowing that your services provide incredible value, which is reflected in your pricing.
- Seizing growth opportunities
  - Instead of missing out, you'll be primed to identify and seize every opportunity. Whether networking, partnerships, or investments, you'll step into them with confidence, knowing they'll enhance your business and income.

Achieving Success Through the Pillars of Body Based Business

Nervous System Regulation

You can regulate your nervous system to achieve results through "in the moment" methods such as yoga, breathwork, and humming. These will be extremely helpful for consistently getting you to a regulated space and cannot be missed. They formulate the foundation of pillar 1 of BBB, regulation. They might include the following:

- Emotional processing tools that will help you identify, validate, express, and release emotional energy from the body, promoting a sense of calm
- Practical strategies you can use with limited time, space, or privacy that will help you shift nervous system states, enhancing feelings of safety and balance
- Grounding practices that bring awareness to the body, helping you stay present and connected
- Breathing techniques designed to calm or activate the nervous system, depending on what type of dysregulation you're experiencing and what 's needed to return to regulation
- Physical activities, routines, and nutrition choices that support energy regulation, reduce stress, and promote resilience

The limitation of these tools is that they don't address the deep-seated psychological reasons behind your dysregulation. Essentially, you can practice regulation techniques like deep breathing every time you receive a triggering email or process emotions repeatedly. But until you address the underlying reason why that email frustrates you, you'll end up exhausting yourself by focusing solely on regulation. Plus, this approach drains energy you could otherwise use for building your business, achieving success, or contributing to your community.

Trauma Healing

The most effective way to find the consistent regulation that makes entrepreneurship as simple and sustainable as it can be is by also addressing the underlying reasons you may become dysregulated. We will do this in pillar 2, trauma healing, by using the latest neuroscience and tried-and-tested reflections and practices. This second pillar is a large part of why the BBB methodology is so effective—because it addresses the underlying reason that you're feeling dysregulated. We'll talk about some of the tools you can use:

- Somatic therapeutic tools such as parts work, somatic experiencing, and inner child work.
- Looking at your attachment style and core wounds in relation to caregivers, money, and sense of self.

Protocols

The third pillar is where everything comes together and you set yourself up for long-term success, as well as more energy and ease. Pillar 3 of BBB, protocols, will give you the systems and protocols that channel and empower your strengths, intuition, and intelligence so that you expend less energy on regulating and healing and more energy on creating the profitable, purposeful business and life you want. We'll talk about tools such as these:

- Emotional regulation, maintaining focus, developing self-discipline, and setting clear objectives
- Effective organization and execution of daily tasks, such as managing emails, scheduling, finances, and other administrative duties to ensure smooth business operations

- Building and maintaining strong, healthy relationships with clients, team members, and stakeholders by using clear communication, empathy, and conflict resolution skills
- Long-term planning and visionary thinking into leadership roles to guide the team and organization toward sustainable growth and innovation
- Managing group dynamics, fostering collaboration, and aligning team members with organizational goals while ensuring their well-being and productivity

EXERCISE: Creating Your Vision

I invited Debbie and Emily to complete this visioning exercise to help them identify what they wanted to accomplish in the program, and I'd like to invite you to do the same. It's easy to read a book and then forget what you've learned unless you clearly name what you want to get out of it and take the steps to reach those goals.

Start setting your intentions and defining what you'd like to gain from this book by answering the following questions:

- Where in your life or business are you currently operating in dysregulation?
- How would your energy, productivity, or well-being shift if you were more attuned to your body's signals and rhythms?
- How could mastering emotional regulation and nervous system resilience improve your leadership, decision-making, and relationships in both your business and personal life?
- What would change in your life if you could build a more sustainable and joyful business?
- What decisions have you been delaying or overthinking?

- How would your life change if you had clarity on what the "right" decision is and the confidence to act on it?
- How would making more aligned, body-based decisions affect your confidence and creativity in growing your business and increasing your income?
- What specific areas of your business feel like they need more ease and flow?

In just this one session, I began to see the two most common ways people respond to this information, as demonstrated by Debbie and Emily.

Debbie quickly recognized that her anxiety and sensitive stomach might be linked to a dysregulated nervous system. She'd already visited the doctor about both issues but hadn't found a solution, so the possibility of a nervous system connection made sense to her. As I described symptoms, particularly those relating to relationships, she found herself nodding along. She'd been feeling distant from her partner, struggling to feel seen and heard, and it seemed they were stuck in repetitive, unproductive conversations. Debbie was also finding it difficult to connect with her son, who had been acting out at school. When she learned that the nervous system only feels safe to connect with others when it's in the ventral vagal (or regulated) state and noticed that she spends a large part of her life dysregulated, she wondered if her difficulty connecting with her son and partner could be because her body struggled to feel safe enough to connect with them authentically.

Emily was also a bit apprehensive but leaned toward curiosity. She was hopeful that regulating her nervous system might lessen her migraines and had already scheduled a yoga session. She also began to wonder how nervous system regulation could impact her relationships. Members in her group were discussing its potential effects, and although her relationship with her partner was stable, she was feeling the strain of balancing work and family life. She'd noticed that when she was calm, her sensitive child tended to have steadier emotions, which made her think this might indeed be tied to her own dysregulation. However, she was pretty sure all of this was due to dysregulation from the busy life she led and made a mental note to ignore the information about deeper emotional work, thinking it wasn't applicable to her.

This session highlighted how individuals like Debbie and Emily each respond uniquely to nervous system regulation, with one focused on specific physical symptoms and the other on broader emotional and relational impacts.

Key Takeaways

- The nervous system constantly processes external and internal stimuli, impacting stress levels, focus, and productivity. When the nervous system is dysregulated, it leads to chronic anxiety, burnout, and decreased decision-making abilities.
- Understanding your nervous system will help you find emotional balance and business growth without sacrificing personal well-being.
- Addressing the root cause of stress in the nervous system is crucial for long-term health and sustained business growth.
- Now that you've created your vision of what you want to get out of this book, you're ready to learn how to access your body's wisdom so you always have an unparalleled guide to decision-making and success.

Chapter 2
Intuition and Somatic Intelligence

By the second session of Body Based Business, Debbie and Emily were facing some big decisions. Debbie had received an application from a potential client that looked wonderful on paper, and Emily was considering signing up for a course on product development but was conflicted.

For Debbie, the problem was that, technically, this new client ticked all the boxes . . . but when she read through the words, she felt her stomach twist. Something seemed off, and she felt a compulsion to cancel the client's initial consultation call. Of course, her mind told her that she couldn't, reasoning that nothing was wrong and that she shouldn't send away good money.

For Emily, the problem was that even though her whole body felt pulled toward this course, she'd promised herself she'd focus on work and stop learning this year. The pull she felt toward the course, combined with this mental chatter, was literally giving her headaches that were about to become full-blown migraines—her sensitivity to light increased every time she sat down with her journal to write a pros-and-cons list. She had an inkling inside that signing up for a course on product development was the next best step, but it was a step away from the path she'd planned for herself and her business. Something wasn't right.

What Debbie and Emily didn't know was that they were beginning to access their somatic intelligence. This is a critical tool for entrepreneurs, as they give access to the body's wisdom and guide decision-making by giving you a more direct, easier way to find your own version of success.

When Debbie arrived at our BBB session, she was scattered and agitated, as she'd spent the morning arguing with her partner instead of preparing for her meetings that day. Emily was also overwhelmed, arriving late as it had taken her longer to get ready that morning with a pounding headache.

I could sense this chaotic energy in the air and invited five complete, deep breaths before we got into the material of the day: somatic intelligence.

Somatic Intelligence

On one hand, most humans have an intuitive understanding that being emotionally aware and in tune with others is crucial for both personal and professional success. However, the term *emotional intelligence* wasn't coined until the 1960s and didn't gain popularity until Daniel Goleman published his book *Emotional Intelligence* in 1995. Today, almost every workplace worldwide recognizes the importance of emotional intelligence and proactively invests time, energy, and effort into improving it.

In this book, we're introducing another layer: somatic intelligence. Somatic intelligence is your personal key to understanding and achieving success. It goes beyond emotions—it involves tuning into your body's wisdom and signals, helping you align your actions and decisions with what your body communicates.

While interpretations may vary, for the purpose of this book, we'll establish a shared understanding. Somatic intelligence, as we'll explore, is the ability to recognize, interpret, and respond to the signals and wisdom of your body. This form of intelligence allows you to deepen your connection to yourself, regulate your nervous system, and navigate the challenges of work and life with greater ease and insight. It is innate to every being and can guide us toward our optimal path of success with the least amount of resistance and most amount of satisfaction, success, peace, ease, and excitement in life.

Just as healthy cells perform their individual roles to help the entire body function at its best capacity, individuals can access that same intelligence to perform their unique jobs in the most effortless and seamless way, supporting their own well-being and that of society. Your somatic intelligence gives you the exact skills and gifts you need and puts you into the exact space you need to occupy to make the impact you need make in this world as we create a more harmonious way of living.

Over time, you'll learn to differentiate between impulses arising from the fear-based, scared, or hurt parts of you and true intuition and somatic intelligence. For now, a general rule of thumb for discerning whether a feeling is intuition or fear is that intuition presents as a soft nudge and knowing. It does not carry force or urgency. In contrast, fear brings a sense of urgency and a "do this or else XYZ will happen" mentality.

The deeper you dive into healing trauma and repeatedly practice being present in your body, the easier it will become to access somatic intelligence instead of fear or pain. However, if you've experienced pain and stress in your life, your body might hold uncomfortable sensations, causing you to avoid being present in your body and to ignore these subtle cues by engaging in behaviors like overeating, overworking, planning excessively, overthinking, undereating, staying busy, or dissociating into Netflix. If this resonates with you, go slowly as you begin to spend more time in your body, and focus heavily on pillar 1 (nervous system regulation).

It might help you to know that somatic intelligence seldom makes logical sense—it goes beyond logic and often makes more sense in hindsight. This is exciting and means there is an incredible array of opportunities you may not even imagine that are available to you! It also requires faith and patience to learn how to read these signals. I encourage you to trust that your body holds a deep wisdom that, when acknowledged and honored, can guide you toward the best outcomes for your life and business.

In my journey of learning to understand and access somatic intelligence, and teaching my clients to do the same, I've found it supports us in many ways. These are some of the most common benefits:

- Somatic intelligence enables swift, informed decisions in time-sensitive situations.
- It sparks creative solutions and innovative ideas.
- Somatic intelligence helps us recognize patterns and connect diverse information.
- It fosters trust, authenticity, and empathy in business relationships.
- Somatic intelligence guides decisions in ambiguous situations, helping us to navigate uncertainty.
- It ensures decisions align with your core values and long-term vision.

EXERCISE: Strengthening Your Intuition Through Somatic Intelligence

Somatic intelligence is clouded and hard to access when our nervous system is in dysregulation, when we are operating from trauma and disempowerment, or when we haven't learned how our personal intelligence communicates through our body. In pillars 1 and 2, you'll learn more about how to decrease the frequency of operating from dysregulation and disempowerment. This exercise will support you in learning the language of your nervous system. By practicing it consistently, you'll become fluent in your body's language over time.

Step 1: Create a quiet space.

- Find a comfortable, quiet place where you won't be disturbed for about ten to fifteen minutes.
- Sit or lie down in a relaxed position, close your eyes, and take a few deep breaths. Inhale deeply through your nose, hold for a moment, and exhale slowly through your mouth.

Step 2: Tune in to your body.

- Begin to bring your awareness to different parts of your body, starting from your toes and moving up to your head. Notice any sensations: warmth, coolness, tingling, tightness, or relaxation. Just observe without judgment of what you think is good, bad, or the correct amount. There is a list below that will help you identify what sensations you might be feeling.
- If you're not sure if you're thinking about what you feel, assuming what you should feel, or truly just feeling, know that's a common experience and totally okay. For now, you can go with what you think you feel, and over time, you'll get a deeper connection to what you feel, and you'll be able to discern when you are thinking about what you feel versus feeling what you feel.

These are some common temperature sensations:

- Warmth—a gentle heat in certain areas, such as the chest, hands, or belly
- Coolness—a slight chill or refreshing cool feeling on the skin or internally

- Heat—intense heat, often localized or spread over the body
- Cold—deep chill, sometimes felt in extremities like hands, feet, or face

These are some common tactile sensations:

- Tingling—prickling or pins-and-needles feeling, often in hands, feet, or face
- Tickle—light, fluttery sensation often causing an urge to laugh or squirm
- Itchiness—an uncomfortable sensation that urges scratching
- Numbness—lack of feeling or sensation, often in the limbs or other areas
- Prickling—sharp, tiny jabs, like being poked with needles
- Softness—gentle, smooth, or cushioned feeling in certain areas

These are some common pressure sensations:

- Heaviness—a dense or weighted feeling in limbs or entire body
- Lightness—a sensation of buoyancy or weightlessness
- Tightness—constricted or compressed feeling, often in chest, throat, or pelvic floor
- Tension—muscular stiffness or strain, common in the neck, back, or jaw
- Contraction—muscles tightening, such as in the abdomen or shoulders
- Expansion—a feeling of spreading or opening, often in the chest or belly

These are some common movement sensations:

- Fluttering—quick, light movements, often felt in the stomach or chest

- Buzzing—a vibration or rapid pulsing, commonly in the limbs or heart area
- Trembling—small, uncontrolled shaking, often from nervousness or fear
- Shakiness—unsteady, jittery feeling throughout the body or specific parts
- Pulsing—rhythmic, heartbeat-like sensation, usually in the temples or extremities
- Waves—rolling or rippling sensations, often through the chest or back

These are some common contraction and release sensations:

- Clenching—tightening or gripping, often in the fists, jaw, or stomach
- Gripping—feeling of holding tightly, particularly in the hands or stomach
- Loosening—a release of tension, allowing the muscles to soften
- Relaxation—a sense of ease and softness throughout the muscles
- Spasms—sudden, involuntary contractions of muscles
- Cramping—painful, squeezing sensation in muscles, such legs or stomach

These are some common energy sensations:

- Calmness—a sense of peace or stillness throughout the body
- Agitation—restless or jittery energy, often causing discomfort
- Energy—a surge of energy, often felt in limbs or chest
- Fatigue—heavy, drained feeling, often throughout the body or in specific areas
- Buzzing—a high-energy, electric feeling often associated with anxiety or excitement

These are some common depth and volume sensations:

- Hollowness—a sense of emptiness, often in the chest or belly
- Fullness—a feeling of being filled, often in the stomach or chest
- Denseness—heaviness or thickness, often associated with fatigue or tension
- Spaciousness—open or free feeling, often experienced in the chest or head

These are some common emotional sensations:

- Butterflies—light, fluttery sensation in the stomach, often from excitement or nerves
- Heart racing—rapid heartbeat, often experienced during fear, anxiety, or excitement
- Heart pounding—strong, forceful beats in the chest
- Constriction—tightness or pressure, often in the throat or chest, linked to anxiety or sadness
- Sinking—a feeling of heaviness or dropping in the chest or belly, often linked to sadness or dread
- Openness—a sense of expansion or vulnerability, often in the heart or chest

These are some common pain-related sensations:

- Ache—a dull, persistent pain, often in muscles or joints
- Burning—a sharp, fiery sensation, often felt in muscles or skin
- Sharpness—a sudden, intense pain, like being poked or stabbed
- Stabbing—intense, localized pain, often sharp and quick
- Throbbing—a rhythmic pain, usually in sync with the heartbeat
- Soreness—a tender or sensitive feeling, often in muscles after exertion

These are some common digestive sensations:

- Gurgling—internal movement in the stomach or intestines, often heard and felt
- Hunger pangs—gnawing or empty feeling in the stomach, linked to hunger
- Nausea—a rolling or unsettled feeling in the stomach, often linked to discomfort
- Bloating—swollen, full feeling in the belly, often from gas or overeating

Step 3: Recall a recent decision.

- Think of a recent decision you made, whether big or small. It could be choosing what to eat for breakfast, deciding to reach out to a friend, or making a business decision. How did you feel in your body when you made that choice? Were there any sensations or feelings that guided you? The goal here is to notice, not mark as right or wrong.
- Reflecting on this decision, were there certain feelings or thoughts that were telling you to take one option over another? For example, you might have a fluttery, excited energy in your chest asking you to message a friend, and you might have a heavy, pulling sensation in your belly encouraging you to pull back and refrain from texting.

Step 4: Explore a current question or decision.

- Now bring to mind a current question or decision you're facing. Don't overthink it—just allow your focus to be whatever comes to mind.
- As you think about this decision, place your hand over your heart or gut and ask yourself "What is my body telling me about this?"

Notice any physical sensations, feelings, or mental images that feel life soft knowings, gut feelings, or whispers. Disregard anything that feels like fear, anxiety, or has any type of urgency. Ask the softer sensation/knowing/feeling "If you could speak, what would you say?" and "If you could act, what would you do?"

- If you struggle to disregard the negative feelings, that's understandable. For now, keep trying this exercise. In pillar 2, you'll learn how to clear away the fear, anxiety, and emotions that cloud your access to your somatic intelligence.

Step 5: Journal your experience.

- Open your eyes and take a moment to journal about your experience. Write down what you noticed in your body: any sensations, feelings, or images that came up. I recommend observing if you have any judgments or if things start to mean something to you. Write those down without fully buying into their meaning. For example, I might experience a buzzing sensation in my chest and have a thought that says, *This is fear.* For the sake of learning about your body, simply observe the judgments you're making and take note of them. In pillar 2, you'll learn more about how to decipher the meanings of the thoughts and sensations you have.

- Reflect on how these insights might guide your decision or action. Consider responding to these questions:
  - Did you receive a clear answer, or do you feel more connected to a particular direction?
  - Did your somatic intelligence communicate with you through a specific sensation or feeling?
  - How does your body's response differ when you consider different options or scenarios?
  - Do you notice a difference in how your body feels when you act on intuitive guidance versus when you ignore it?

Step 6: Practice regularly.

- Somatic intelligence strengthens with consistent connection and practice. Make a habit of checking in with your body before making decisions, no matter how small. The more you practice, the more easily you'll recognize the subtle cues that guide you. Start by doing it two to three times a week and work your way up to doing it every day.

Once Debbie and Emily had each completed this exercise, they felt more connected to specific directions in response to their individual decisions. However, they both had very different responses to this connection.

Debbie worried that her inner voice might be wrong and that she was "being dramatic," so she chose to work with the client anyway. After their initial onboarding session, things felt tense, but Debbie rationalized that since the money was good, it was worth it, so she pushed through. Her sensitive stomach flared up more regularly, putting her in a bad mood, which had a ripple effect on her relationship and parenting, making both her partner and her child feel ignored and unloved.

On the other hand, Emily's somatic intelligence encouraged her to go ahead with the course, and she chose to listen by signing up that afternoon. In the course's first session, she met an Ayurvedic practitioner who introduced her to an herbal remedy for her migraines which began to work wonders! As a result, she had extra energy and space to give more intention to her relationship with her partner, who had started hinting at a possible engagement in the future. She felt the benefits of this improvement even more when her child began sharing more openly about what was happening at school, as a result of Emily being much more present with her in the evenings.

Key Takeaways

- Somatic intelligence is the innate body wisdom that helps align with your values and purpose.
- It can sometimes be referred to as intuition.
- It is a powerful guide for quick decision-making, creativity, and connection.
- Trauma and stress cloud access to this wisdom, but with practice, you can strengthen your connection to your body.

Now that you've practiced (and are continuing to practice!) strengthening your intuition through somatic intelligence, you are ready to learn how nervous system dysregulation is blocking your intuition—and how to gain more access to it.

Chapter 3
Identifying Your Dysregulation

Debbie and Emily were overwhelmed and looking for proof of concept and sustainability in their business ideas.

Debbie's stomach issues had worsened, with frequent bloating, cramping, and unpredictable trips to the bathroom disrupting her days, signaling her IBS was becoming severe. She found herself constantly rehearsing responses in her head, double-checking emails, and overpreparing for meetings, all in an effort to appear knowledgeable and credible. Between these efforts, she was researching her audience obsessively, trying to convince herself that her business idea had staying power. Because of the constant energy expended worrying about what other people were thinking, she felt she needed extra time to herself which made her partner and child feel even more alone.

Emily was also anxious about others' opinions, but her fear of failure ran deeper, consuming her thoughts. She'd make progress on a project, only to get sidetracked, then avoid the work altogether—though she hadn't yet recognized fear as the root of this pattern. Her body was carrying the weight of her stress, building tension that showed up as persistent back pain, which even her regular yoga sessions couldn't relieve. She felt an eerie sense of dread that she hadn't experienced since childhood, as if something was about to go terribly wrong and fall apart. The feeling gnawed at her, yet she couldn't pinpoint what was wrong—maybe everything?

What Debbie and Emily didn't see at this time was that these physical, mental, and emotional responses weren't a sign of something actually being wrong, but rather a result of their nervous systems experiencing constant, chronic dysregulation. When they sat down at our regular session, they were buzzing with anticipation and hope that they'd find a way to ease the stress. The most important place to start was with the self-diagnosis quiz.

EXERCISE: Self-Diagnosis Quiz

Right now, there aren't any really solid, all-encompassing tests for nervous system dysregulation that scientists have fully validated. Plus, no test or self-assessment can perfectly capture your whole personality or give a complete picture of what you're going through right now, whether it's in your personal life or in your business.

However, this self-diagnosis quiz will help you discern how much of your current experience with entrepreneurship is being impacted by a dysregulated nervous system and, therefore, what you need in order to find your path to easeful success, defined as avoiding burnout, working within your values, and leaving an impact.

Disclaimer on Stress

There's a difference between natural stress symptoms and nervous system dysregulation. It's normal and expected for a healthy human to respond with some of the symptoms in the quiz when you're going through temporary stressful periods. So, if you've only been dealing with symptoms for a few days or weeks, and they're not seriously affecting you, your nervous system might just be in a temporary high-stress mode but not necessarily dysregulated. Once things calm down, your nervous system should naturally return to a more relaxed state, and your body will take care of any short-term stress effects.

However, if your symptoms have been hanging around for more than a few weeks or months, it could be a sign that your nervous system is starting to tend toward dysregulation. Even if things feel manageable now, without doing something to get your nervous system back to a set point of regulation, your dysregulation (and symptoms) could get worse over time. Now is the perfect moment to dive into this book and start the Body Based Business method. It'll help you relieve the current symptoms, start repairing any damage, and stop any more issues from piling up.

Instructions

1. Read each statement carefully.
2. Rate how frequently each statement applies to you using the following scale:
   0 = Never
   1 = Rarely
   2 = Sometimes
   3 = Often
   4 = Always
3. At the end, tally your score to understand your results.

Disclaimer: This quiz is for educational purposes only and is not a substitute for professional medical or psychological advice. If you have concerns about your mental or physical health, please consult a qualified healthcare provider.

Quiz Questions

1. I feel overwhelmed by the amount of work I have to do in my business.
   Rating ____

2. I find it difficult to make important decisions quickly and confidently.
   Rating ____

3. I procrastinate on tasks that are crucial for my business growth.
   Rating ____

4. When faced with unexpected challenges, I feel panicked or anxious.
   Rating ____

5. I have trouble sleeping because I'm constantly thinking about my business.
   Rating ____

6. I experience physical symptoms (e.g., headaches, muscle tension, digestive issues) during stressful business periods.
   Rating ____

7. I avoid taking risks in my business due to fear of failure or uncertainty.
   Rating ____

8. I find it hard to focus and stay productive throughout the day.
   Rating ____

9. I react strongly to criticism or negative feedback about my business.
   Rating ____

10. I feel the need to control every aspect of my business and struggle with delegating tasks.
    Rating ____

11. I struggle to disconnect and relax, even during my personal time.
    Rating ____

12. I doubt my abilities and feel like an impostor in my field.
    Rating ____

13. I notice mood swings that correlate with the ups and downs of my business.
    Rating ____

14. I have difficulty setting and maintaining healthy boundaries with clients, employees, or partners.
    Rating ____

15. I replay past mistakes in my mind and have trouble moving past them.
    Rating ____

16. I experience physical symptoms that have not been successfully addressed by traditional medical systems.
    Rating ____

17. I walk through life experiencing an underlying background sense of anxiety and worry.
    Rating ____

18. I feel low energy and disengaged, without much sense of purpose or meaning, like life is passing me by.
    Rating ____

19. I experience some of the following symptoms:
    o Anxiety (health anxiety, high-functioning anxiety, social anxiety, etc.)
    o Autoimmune conditions
    o Nervous system disorders such as POTS
    o Burnout, chronic fatigue, or fibromyalgia
    o Chronic pain
    o Digestive issues like IBS, stress-related gut problems
    o Panic attacks, phobias
    o Sleep disorders like insomnia
    o Tension and pain I can't relieve despite trying such as chronic UTI's or jaw clenching

    Rating ___

20. I feel that nothing I ever do is enough and think I should be doing more.

    Rating ___

21. After achieving financial goals, I go on spending sprees, buying things I don't need or even want.

    Rating ___

Scoring

- Add up your ratings for all twenty-one questions to get your total score.

    Total Score ___

Results Interpretation

0–25 points

Your nervous system responses have a minimal impact on your entrepreneurial journey. You likely have effective coping mechanisms and resilience strategies in place. Continue to nurture these strengths and remain attentive to your well-being. However, if your symptoms have been hanging around for more than a few weeks or months, it could be a sign that your nervous system is starting to tend toward dysregulation. Even if things feel manageable now, without doing something to get your nervous system back to a set point of regulation, your dysregulation (and symptoms) could get worse over time. Now is the perfect moment to dive into the BBB protocol. It'll help you relieve the current symptoms, start repairing any damage, and stop any more issues from piling up.

25–50 points

Your moderate nervous system dysregulation, stress, and overwhelm are frequently impacting your decisions and productivity. You might be struggling to fall or stay asleep (maybe you need a glass of wine or melatonin to sleep well). You might feel tired and anxious during the day and your emotions might feel like a lot to handle, meaning life often just feels like A LOT! If you're overwhelmed by life's stressors and needing extra time alone or with people who make you feel safe just to get through each day, you're in the right place.

Physically, this dysregulation might manifest as inflammation or tension, leading to chronic pain in areas like your shoulders or back. It could even contribute to more serious conditions, like rheumatoid arthritis, IBS, or depression. You might also find that you're particularly sensitive to things like loud noises or bright fluorescent lights, which can feel especially stressful or uncomfortable.

51+ points

You're dealing with a lot of stress, anxiety, or feeling constantly out of balance, and it's holding you back from effectively growing your business— which is a really hard place to be. I've been there, and I know it can feel really exhausting sometimes.

Daily tasks might feel like climbing a mountain, and you could be dealing with one or more health diagnoses on top of that. Getting a good night's sleep might feel like a rare luxury, and it's possible that you've been struggling just to feel okay for years. You might find that things others don't even blink at, like certain lights, sounds, or textures, make you feel even worse.

If that sounds like you, I'm really glad you're here. I wrote this book to help you. It's important to take things slow on your healing journey—no need to rush. Your heightened sensitivity gives you a stronger connection to your somatic intelligence which will become your superpower in your business, something that others might even be a bit envious of.

In addition to this book, it might be worth looking into getting some support from professionals who specialize in nervous system regulation, somatic therapies, or stress management. That professional support might be coaching with me (sheridanruth.com will have info on that), or you may have another type of support that feels really good to you. Go with what feels best.

At the root of all these different symptoms is one underlying cause a dysregulated nervous system that has lost its ability to flexibly respond to stressors, and as a result, the creative energy required to pursue entrepreneurship sustainably is wrapped up in surviving the day-to-day.

Common Barriers to Implementing Nervous System Regulation

When implementing this information, there's a common pitfall: many people fall into perfectionism, using nervous system regulation as another way to judge, shame, and "fix" themselves. Approaching these practices with an underlying desire to fix yourself actually reinforces low self-esteem, shame, and nervous system dysregulation.

It's a tricky cycle—wanting to use this information to make life easier and improve mental and physical health, but having a perfectionist mindset that disrupts that desire by creating a dysregulated nervous system. At first, I noticed this pattern in my clients (and myself) and thought it was just a quirky habit we had. But scientific studies actually support that perfectionism creates a dysregulated nervous system, which can heighten sensitivity to stress and lead to depression.[2]

Breaking it down, perfectionism stems from an inner belief or feeling that there is something wrong with you that needs fixing. If you believe there's something inherently wrong, your body senses this as a threat to belonging and security. It's as if your body is saying "If others see something wrong with me, they'll reject me!" In response, it activates stress responses to direct energy toward fixing the perceived threat (you). This stress response fills your body with cortisol, a stress hormone that prepares you to confront or escape perceived threats.

---

2. Hanna Suh, Pey-Yan Liou, Jisun Jeong, and Shin Ye Kim, "Perfectionism, Prolonged Stress Reactivity, and Depression: A Two-Wave Cross-Lagged Analysis," *Journal of Rational-Emotive & Cognitive-Behavior Therapy* (2022): 1–15, https://doi.org/10.1007/s10942-022-00483-x.

Since your body can't achieve its goal of fixing you, the cortisol remains, keeping you from returning to a regulated state. Living in this perpetual stress state, you always feel something is wrong, which fuels the perfectionist, increases stress responses, and can lead to self-criticism, chronic health issues, and depression. Honestly, it's exhausting even to describe.

Instead, when you approach this work with self-compassion and curiosity, you shift from a defensive state (protecting yourself from the perceived threat of rejection) to activating the qualities of a regulated nervous system. To prevent adding dysregulation while trying to reduce it, seek out ways to practice self-compassion and curiosity as you move through this work. This approach creates an upward spiral of well-being rather than a downward spiral of stress. We call this "practice over perfection," emphasizing the importance of showing up to practice regulation, rather than stressing about getting it right.

Debbie and Emily had completed the quiz, listened carefully to my reflections on compassion and curiosity, and, as they had in every session so far, responded in dramatically different ways.

Debbie zoned out when she heard about compassion and curiosity, thinking *I tried that before…it didn't work…nope.* She left the session determined to get this right and regulate her nervous system perfectly. She noted down all the things she could do to get "better," texted her friend Belinda about it, and sent her the link to the quiz. Her friend quickly replied, "Lol, this is pseudoscience—you're fine." Ouch. Debbie wanted to crawl into her skin. She ripped up her plans but couldn't shake the nagging feeling that something needed fixing within her—and that if she didn't fix it, she'd be failing yet again and dooming her business to fail. Over the next three months, she lingered in actions toward looking for proof of concept, feeling more and more like a failure and increasingly behind. Everything came to a head when her child got into trouble at school and didn't tell her. When she found out, Debbie exploded, yelling at her child, who recoiled, put her headphones on, and refused to talk about it anymore.

Emily also made a long list of all the ways she felt dysregulated, but she wrote in big, bold letters at the top: Practice over Perfection. She made a commitment to herself to simply notice where she was dysregulated, show up for the next session, and learn more. This felt good and grounding, though a little scary, as part of her thought she should be doing more. Then, that evening at yoga, something shifted. She had been practicing yoga for years and had always wanted to master crow pose (an inversion where you lift your knees onto your triceps and balance on your hands) but had never quite been able to do it. She'd continued practicing without fixating on crow pose, and recently, she'd been practicing yoga even more. So that evening, when the instructor cued crow pose, she tried again— and nailed it! She hovered in the air for nearly a full minute. This success reinforced her belief that it's about showing up to the practice, not pushing toward perfection. She realized that when you practice, you get there; when you push, you don't.

She ran home to share her realization about practice over perfection with her partner and child, and they had an amazing evening together. Her partner continued to secretly plan a proposal, feeling inspired by Emily's excitement. Emily leaned further into the idea that nothing was wrong with her—her nervous system was simply dysregulated. This understanding gave her the energy and clarity to complete her financial forecasting and gain all the information she needed to feel confident she had proof of concept for her new product.

Key Takeaways

- By taking this self-diagnosis quiz, you will be able to identify if a dysregulated nervous system is impacting your entrepreneurial experience, though temporary stress does not necessarily indicate long-term dysregulation.
- Perfectionism and survival states often trigger more stress and self-criticism, leading to dysregulation and creating a cycle of increased cortisol and stress-related health issues.
- Shifting focus to curiosity and self-compassion will reduce stress, promote nervous system regulation, and encourage sustainable growth through consistent practice rather than perfection.

Now that you've identified your patterns of dysregulation, you are ready to learn how your nervous system shapes your perception of reality and how to see it more clearly.

Pillar 1: Nervous System Regulation

At 2:00 a.m., both Debbie and Emily were lying in bed, feeling their hearts pound while their minds raced with plans, worries, and ideas for their businesses. With their notes apps open, they hid the glow of their screens from their partners and jotted down endless to-do lists, ideas, and plans. Each time their bodies felt heavy and almost drifted into sleep, a new thought would pop up, jolting them awake and sending them spiraling for another fifteen minutes. This cycle repeated until sunrise, leaving them starting the day frustrated, anxious, and on the verge of tears.

Debbie hadn't dealt with insomnia like this in years, while Emily, though often struggling with sleep, had never felt this scattered at such a late hour. After nights of trying every wellness hack—cutting caffeine, no phones in bed, trying melatonin and magnesium supplements—they showed up at the coffee shop by our session's room with swollen, tired eyes. Debbie joked to Emily, "Eleven a.m. and we're on coffee number two! Why are we so tired?" What they weren't aware of was that their insomnia had flared up due to nervous system dysregulation.

For Debbie and Emily, this lack of sleep seemed normal. Building a business, leading, and being a founder were hard work, so a bit of stress and sleeplessness made sense—especially in today's economy, right? Well . . . yes and no.

The hardships Debbie and Emily were experiencing were due to unnecessary stress caused by their dysregulated nervous systems. They didn't realize that a regulated nervous system could manage the challenges of entrepreneurship without making it feel like the world was falling apart or significantly impacting their well-being. Sure, entrepreneurship would always bring challenges, but not so exhausting that it would consistently rob them of sleep. Part of the reason their nervous systems were so dysregulated had little to do with them and everything to do with the very nature of entrepreneurship.

Your nervous system perceives entrepreneurship as a threat because it involves uncertainty, exposes you to judgment, and often requires you to approach things differently from others. Trying to stay positive, create change, or maintain a wise perspective is nearly impossible when your body believes it's fighting for survival. Additionally, part of the exhaustion and burnout you may experience comes from working in a state of dysregulation. It's hard to connect with your somatic intelligence and build confidence in it when you can't even hear it—your body is too busy preparing to run from a bear.

On the flip side, a regulated nervous system can handle stress—whether it's a sudden event like a loud noise, or an ongoing challenge like juggling a busy workload—without worsening physical and emotional symptoms. It becomes adaptable enough to handle emotional stressors like a breakup or physical ones like fighting a cold while meeting a client deadline. When regulated, the nervous system can activate energy for focus and then dial it back down, allowing for natural relaxation, restful sleep, and a clear mind ready to handle challenges like unhappy customers.

By learning to regulate your nervous system using the information in the following chapters, you can expect these positive results:

- You'll be able to deal with the challenges of entrepreneurship more effectively.
- You'll have more energy for your day-to-day work.
- You'll prevent burnout.
- You'll understand that the key to easeful entrepreneurship isn't through avoiding stressful situations but by learning how to leverage them to increase your healt
- You'll learn how to hear and access your secret weapon to purpose and profit—somatic intelligence.

Chapter 4
Crisis Averted—Learning to Regulate

After a sleepless night, Debbie was quickly spooning muesli into her mouth when she glanced at her phone and saw an email from a client requesting a refund. The client was dissatisfied with her deliverables, and the words on the screen seemed to blur as Debbie felt an instant knot in her stomach. A familiar surge of anxiety washed over her—her heart sped up, and her hands started to shake. Her mind zeroed in on the email, blocking everything else out, and she felt an intense need to respond immediately to fix things.

Her first instinct was to fight, so she started drafting a long, defensive response, trying to justify her work and prove herself right. But as she typed, doubt began creeping in. What if the client wouldn't see her perspective? What if no explanation would satisfy them? Overwhelmed by the thought that she couldn't win this battle, her body slipped into fawn mode (also known as the blue zone or a version of dorsal vagal collapse). Her body's perception of the situation shifted: appeasing, rather than standing her ground, felt safer.

As this fawning response took over, her thoughts spiraled downward: *Of course, I'm not qualified for this.* Self-doubt flooded her mind, and a deep sense of defeat weighed her down. Her shoulders slumped, her stomach dropped, and a wave of hopelessness set in. *Maybe I should just quit for good*, she thought. She swiped the email app closed, crawled into bed, and feeling completely collapsed, numbly scrolled through social media, trying to distract herself from the mounting dread.

Debbie didn't realize that her struggle to handle the refund constructively, connect with the client effectively, or even think creatively about a solution that could benefit her business and allow her to grow from the experience stemmed from the dysregulation triggered by the event. Her nervous system interpreted the refund request as a threat not only to her reputation (her "place in the tribe" from a primal nervous system perspective) but also to her financial security, which she associated with survival and stability.

The promise and hope of care and advice from her BBB session were what pulled her out of bed. When she arrived at her session, she shared the experience with me, asking for advice. I was sympathetic and reassured her that that day's class was perfect for what she was going through. That day, I had planned to introduce the Nervous System Cheat Sheet, and it was clear Debbie was ready.

The Nervous System Cheat Sheet is the number one most popular resource among my clients. It was created in response to clients repeatedly asking "But how do I regulate when I don't have much time, space, or privacy?" This cheat sheet will teach you exactly how to regulate effectively in those moments while also providing deeper insight into how nervous system regulation functions in your body.

EXERCISE: Utilizing the Nervous System Cheat Sheet

The purpose of this cheat sheet is to give you tools that require very little time, energy, space, and privacy to help you feel more calm, grounded, safe and peaceful during the day—even when there is a lot going on.

For the sake of this cheat sheet, that feeling of being safe and easeful is what we call a regulated nervous system and it's related to the green zone.

While this cheat sheet isn't a full list of all the tools and modalities you can use, it's created for you to download to your phone and use when you don't have much time, space, or privacy.

So, your first step? Download it to your phone right now by accessing the most up-to-date, colorful, downloadable PDF at sheridanruth.com/regulate. You'll thank me later. After you download it to your phone, continue reading to understand how to implement the tools.

As mentioned prior, your goal is to spend as much time as possible in the green zone (i.e., a regulated nervous system) without getting upset at yourself when you go into the red, yellow, or blue zones. Anytime you're not in the green zone, you're either in the red, yellow, or blue zones.

These zones are where your body goes when it perceives a threat. This is called a stress response, and it means your body is using its tools to keep you safe! (It's also referred to as a primal response. Meaning, our nervous system isn't aware of the difference between an email from your boss or a bear chasing you through the woods; it reacts the same way.)

Your job is to slowly implement the tools in this PDF to remind the body that it is safe—even when you get emails that make you want to throw your phone at the wall, or your partner is infuriating you.

Understanding the Zones

The primary goal of this cheat sheet is to assist you in reaching the green zone as frequently as possible. **To achieve this, it's crucial to first**

identify which zone you are currently in before utilizing the tools provided. This understanding will enable you to apply the appropriate strategies that will best support your self-regulation.

Each zone (blue, yellow, red, and green) is associated with specific looks, feelings, and responses. By assessing your appearance and emotional state, you will be guided toward the most suitable response to find your way back to self-regulation as efficiently as you can.

Below, you will find a breakdown of each zone, including its corresponding looks, feelings, and responses.

The Blue Zone

- **How I look**—sleepy, dissociating, numb, weak muscles, limp limbs, low energy, mumbling or silent, heart and breath rates slowing, lack of eye contact
- **How I feel**—like I'm going through the motions, dissociated, shamed, threatened, and shutting down. I feel hopeless, out of control, or trapped. "I can't do this." Drained, lethargic, tired, wanting to give up and be alone. I've got emotional constriction or depression.
- **How I respond**—blue zone regulation tools

The Yellow Zone

- **How I look**—tense muscles, heart and breath rates fast and shallow or holding breath, fidgety, volume of voice quieter, looking for an exit, lack of eye contact
- **How I feel**—threatened, defensive, anxious, panicky, worried or fearful. "I want to escape!" Hyperalert or hypervigilant. "I should

do." "I'm not doing enough." "I must push through." Increased heart rate or pounding sensation in the head.

- **How I respond**—yellow zone regulation tools

The Red Zone

- **How I look**—tense muscles, louder voice volume, heart and breath rates increasing, like "I have to move or get out"
- **How I feel**—I feel threatened, angry, frustrated, irritated or annoyed. "I can fight!" Aggressive or dissociative rage, and if I stay here for a while I feel heavy and tired.
- **How I respond**—red zone regulation tools

The Green Zone

- **How I look**—calm, relaxed muscles, normal voice volume, heart and breath rates normal, able to make eye contact and notice breath
- **How I feel**—safe enough, grounded and in the body. I can play, be spontaneous, and go with the flow. I have access to clarity and logical thinking. I feel confident and courageous and meet the demands of my day. "I can do hard things." I feel curious and nonjudgmental. I have access to compassion for myself and others. I feel connected to myself and others. I can make conscious choices, and I can communicate clearly.
- **How I respond**—allow yourself to feel it a little more, to an extent that feels good. If it stops feeling good to be here, that's okay! Let it go. You'll come back to it later. Rest and recharge. Connect with others. Engage in hobbies or other creative and playful activities.

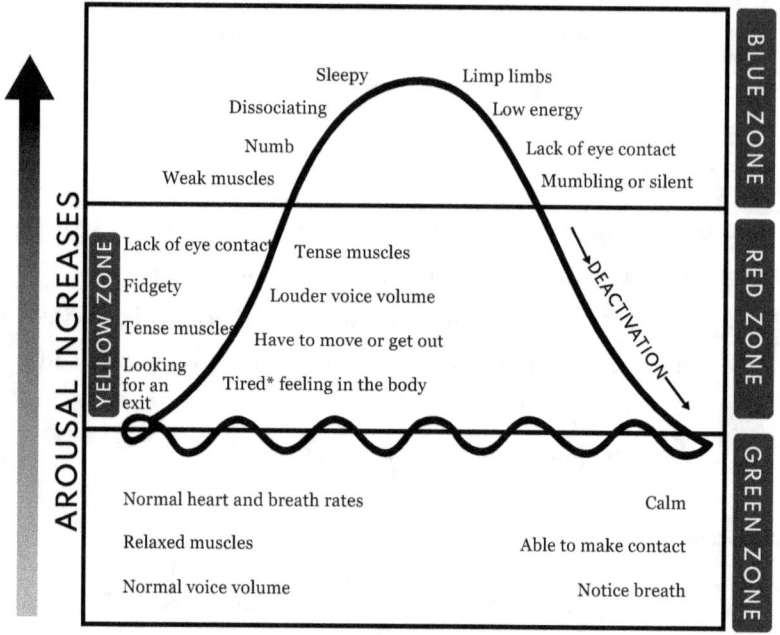

This visual representation demonstrates the symptoms of being in either the red, blue, yellow, or green zones.

Regulating from the Blue Zone

The intention is to move your nervous system into regulation, helping it pull your body's energy back through the body into your limbs and organs. In the image above you can see that the curve from the blue zone goes through the red zone before it gets to the green zone; this means that we have to activate the sympathetic branch of the nervous system to get you back to regulation (the green zone). This doesn't mean we're activating a stress state like flight or fight (yellow and red zones), it just means you can focus on answering the question "How do I fill my body with energy?" By mobilizing energy in your body, you will take your nervous system through the red zone so that it can go from blue to green.

Physical Activities

- Take a walk.
- Do yoga or other gentle movements.
- Run hands and wrists under cold water.
- Press feet flat on the floor.
- Carry heavy things or push heavy things around.
- Go outside.

Breathing and Relaxation Techniques

- Inhale to the count of six, and exhale to the count of four. Having your inhale longer than your exhale helps activate the sympathetic nervous system, which is the pathway to regulation from the blue zone.
- Drink cold water.
- Apply deep pressure to arms and legs (you can slowly apply pressure down arms and legs in a long stroking motion).
- Take a shower. Ideally, a cold shower will help activate your nervous system, but if that feels like too much of a challenge (it usually is for me!), go with a nice warm shower and focus feeling the water on your hands, feet, neck, and back.

Sensory and Creative Expression

- Chew bubblegum.
- Play with sensory sand or Play-Doh.
- Sit with weighted items on your lap.
- Use activating essential oils (citrus, peppermint, etc.).

Regulating in the Yellow Zone

The intention is to release muscle tension and connect to a long exhale, which will activate your parasympathetic branch and your ventral vagal response.

Physical Activities

- Clench and release all of your muscle groups. You can focus on muscles that are already relaxed or those that have tension in them. I recommend you focus on the muscles in your limbs such as glutes, quads, biceps and hands as this mimics the primal process your body wants to go through. (It thinks it's running from a bear when it's in dysregulation, so if you can help it complete the process it wants to complete—movement of some sort—it will be able to bring you back to regulation.)
- Do "heavy work" such as shoveling snow or cleaning.
- Go for a walk—it'll be even more effective if you walk at a brisk pace.
- Squeeze a stress ball as hard as possible, release, and repeat.
- Rip up paper.
- Run up and down steps.
- Doodle on paper (this one can be a bit more distracting, but sometimes works).

Breathing and Relaxation Techniques

- Extend exhalation.
- Practice deep and slow breathing.
- Use calming essential oils (such as lavender or vetiver).
- Drink hot herbal tea such as chamomile.

Sensory and Creative Expression

- Listen to soothing music.
- Talk, write, or make art about what you're feeling.
- Play music by Mozart in the background.

Regulating in the Red Zone

The intention is to express your energy and then bring calm grounding to your body.

- Shake your entire body! Get all the energy moving and out! I recommend doing this for three to twenty minutes. The longer, the better. Start by committing to three minutes, and if you feel like you want to keep going—do it!
- Rock your body back and forth.
- Shake your head quickly. If you can't commit to the full body shake to expel the dysregulated energy, shaking your head can give you similar effects in a more accessible way. I usually recommend using this one when you're in a public place and would only recommend doing it for ten to sixty seconds.
- Rub on your skin or clothing. What we're doing here is bringing your senses into the picture and showing them that things are safe. (If you can rub your body, you're not being threatened by a bear.) You can do it gently or vigorously—whatever feels best to you.
- Move, move, move—any way that feels good to your body.
- Cross-the-line exercises connect the left and right parts of your body, such as tapping left hand to right knee and right hand to left knee, yoga, or alternative nostril breathing.

Breathing and Relaxation Techniques

- Elongate your exhalation by breathing out for the count of six, and in for the count of four. This activates the parasympathetic nervous system and will bring you down into the green zone.
- Practice deep and slow breathing.
- Listen to soothing music.
- Drink hot herbal tea such as chamomile.
- Lie on the floor with your legs up the wall (with or without a weighted eye mask). The weighted eye mask can feel relaxing for some people, and some people find it grounding to have darkness and feel the pressure on their face.
- Have a cold shower.
- Dim the lights.
- Put a cold washcloth on your face.
- Sensory and Creative Expression
- Talk, write, or make art.
- Use calming essential oils (such as lavender or vetiver).
- Doodle on paper.
- Connect with your five senses. Notice the sounds, sights, smells, textures, and tastes around you. This will help your nervous system see that there is no current threat.

Social and Co-Regulation

- Enlist the help of a support person for co-regulation. This is called co-regulation and the connection with another person will help send the message to the body that it's safe and there is another person to protect it if something dangerous were to happen.
- Describe what is happening in your body out loud: "My tummy is going in circles" or "My legs feel heavy." The combination of

labeling your experience, saying it out loud, and hearing it engages more parts of your brain and senses and helps your nervous system see that there is no current threat.

Regulation Activities That Work for More Than One Zone

Physical Activities that Work for the Red and Yellow Zone

- Clench and release muscle groups. You can focus on muscles that are already relaxed, or those that have tension in them. I recommend you focus on the muscles in your limbs such as glutes, quads, biceps, and hands as this mimics the primal process your body want to go through. (It thinks it's running from a bear when it's in dysregulation so if you can help it complete the process it wants to complete—movement of some sort—it will be able to bring you back to regulation.)
- Do "heavy work" such as shoveling snow or cleaning.
- Go for a walk—it'll be even more effective if you walk at a brisk pace.
- Squeeze a stress ball or fidget with Play-Doh.
- Rip up paper.
- Run up and down steps.

Physical Activities for All Zones

- Get up and do something outside. This could be something like a five-minute walk or picking up some eggs from the corner store. We're looking to get you outside and physically out of the environment you are in. The change in scenery along with the movement of your body will hint to your nervous system that you are safe.
- Engage in cross-the-line exercises. Cross-the-line exercises involve crossing your right hand or foot over the center of your

body to the opposite side, followed by your left hand or foot doing the same, which activates both sides of the brain for more holistic brain function and supports nervous system regulation. Practices like yoga and certain forms of dance incorporate these movements, but a simple example is sitting in a chair with both feet on the ground and alternately placing your right hand on your left shoulder and then your left hand on your right shoulder, repeating for five minutes to promote balance and calm.

Social and Co-Regulation for All Zones

- Enlist the help of a support person for co-regulation.
- Get social. (Even if you don't want to!)

Regulation for All Zones When Nothing Works

If you've tried all the techniques and still feel dysregulated, or if your problems just feel too big, you probably need some fun. Seriously—let go, find a novel experience, and have some fun. Fun experiences provide a pattern interrupt, helping your brain break out of stress cycles, boost mood, and increase adaptability. Engaging in new or creative activities also stimulates the vagus nerve, calming the body. Try a new sport, walk in a different park, listen to music you wouldn't normally choose, or pick up a book outside your usual genre. You get bonus points if you do it with someone you love as studies show us that engaging in fun activities with a loved one releases oxytocin, often referred to as the "love hormone," which reduces cortisol and shifts the nervous system to a regulated state.[3]

Debbie immediately downloaded the Nervous System Cheat Sheet to her phone and made a three-step plan to regulate daily. However, true to her tendencies, her drive for perfection quickly turned into self-

---

3. Stephen W. Porges, *The Polyvagal Theory: Neurophysiological Foundations of Emotions, Attachment, Communication, and Self-Regulation* (W.W. Norton & Company, 2011).

imposed pressure. She found herself obsessing over doing it "right" and, overwhelmed, within a week, she'd stopped looking at it, thinking, *If I can't do it well, I won't do it at all.*

Emily took a different approach. Later that day, she got a similar client email, and a sharp pang of anxiety rose in her chest. She quickly reached for her Nervous System Cheat Sheet PDF, opened it on her screen, and scanned the table. Her breathing steadied as she found her current state and chose a cross-the-line exercise, pressing one hand firmly across her body to her opposite shoulder, then switching sides in a rhythmic motion. The tension in her chest softened, her mind sharpened, and she felt grounded again.

With clarity restored, Emily returned to the email. Calmly, she typed out a response, balancing her client's needs with her own boundaries; she kept it honest and supportive without bending over backward. She hit Send, closed her laptop, and felt an immense sense of ease wash over her. That night, for the first time in weeks, she fell into a deep, undisturbed sleep, her mind finally at rest.

Key Takeaways

- When you're in a state of nervous system dysregulation, it's difficult to make wise decisions or access your somatic intelligence, as your body perceives stress like a life-and-death threat.
- Regulating your nervous system allows you to handle the challenges of entrepreneurship with more ease, conserving energy, preventing burnout, and making decisions with clarity and confidence.

- Learning to access your somatic intelligence will help you navigate stress and align your responses to situations with your core values, ensuring more thoughtful and effective actions.

Integrate this into your life and business by downloading the Nervous System Cheat Sheet PDF at sheridanruth.com/regulate. This will help you learn how your nervous system shapes your perception of reality and how to see it more clearly, preparing you for the next step: seeing your nervous system stories.

Chapter 5
Nervous System Stories

Debbie felt a familiar tension as she read a client's email about the project budget. Instantly, her chest tightened, and her mind spiraled. *I'm sure they want to cancel. They won't move ahead with the project. They're going to tell others I'm too expensive.* With each thought, her fear deepened—she began worrying that she might not secure enough clients to feel financially safe. This fear pushed her into "fight" mode. She immediately started overworking, offering extra services at no charge to keep the client happy, depleting her energy, and losing sight of her bigger goals.

Emily found herself stuck in a loop while working on a proposal for a client she really respected and was excited to work with. Each draft felt inadequate, feeding a wave of self-doubt every time she reviewed her work. *They're going to think I'm incapable. They'll see this was a fluke, and realize other firms are more experienced than we are,* she thought. Her nervous system interpreted this as a threat to her competence and identity, putting her into "freeze" mode. She procrastinated, doubted her instincts, and rewrote endlessly, caught in the belief that her worth was entirely tied to the client's approval.

What Debbie and Emily didn't realize was that these anxious thought cycles weren't grounded in the reality of the situation; they were stories created by their nervous systems. These thoughts and feelings, however real they seemed (and they seemed *very* real), were simply protective stories meant to shield them from perceived threats—but the approach wasn't working.

Both arrived at the BBB session with these stories bouncing around their minds. When they sat down in class, they noticed that the sentence on the board read "Your nervous system creates thoughts that shape your perception of reality. When you can untangle from the stress response, you can see reality more clearly." Debbie and Emily pulled out their notebooks to start writing as I began to explain.

Nervous System Stories

Considering 80% of the information you receive about the world comes from what your body communicates to your brain, your mental and emotional states are largely determined by your nervous system's understanding of the world. This means that physical states (like heart rate, breathing patterns, and muscle tension) and emotional and mental states (like feeling sad, angry, happy, or hesitant about something) are both created by your nervous system state and create your nervous system state—it's a bidirectional relationship.[4] We can begin to influence this relationship to create a state of ease, peace, clarity, and confidence in your body, emotions, and mind by understanding your current nervous system stories.

A nervous system story is the narrative your brain constructs based on the signals it receives from your body's physiological and emotional states. These stories shape how you interpret and perceive reality, especially

---

4. Hevel, Derek J., Philip H. F. Kao, Shevaun D. Neupert, and Jason C. Allaire. "Acute Bidirectional Relations Between Affect, Physical Feeling States, and Activity-Related Behaviors Among Older Adults: An Ecological Momentary Assessment Study." *Annals of Behavioral Medicine* 55, no. 1 (2021): 41–50. https://doi.org/10.1093/abm/kaaa008.

under stress or emotional strain. These stories are based on your past experiences, cultural factors, and beliefs, and they have one goal: to help you navigate your reality.[5] The brain combines these signals into thoughts, emotions, and impulses, which may not accurately represent objective reality, but rather reflect how the nervous system, shaped by past experiences, cultural background, and immediate surroundings, interprets the environment.

Nervous system stories are created in three steps:

1. Your body picks up clues (neuroception).
    o   Let's say you open your inbox, and there it is—an email from a client with the subject line, "We Need to Talk." Before you've even read the message, your body is already reacting. This is neuroception, your nervous system's behind-the-scenes radar, constantly scanning for safety or danger. Without you even realizing it, your body picks up on the vague subject line and shifts into alert mode. Why? Because uncertainty is seen as unsafe to your nervous system, and your body and mind probably have past experiences of either hearing those words, saying them to someone else, or witnessing someone receive them, and then having an emotionally charged conversation afterward. So, your heart starts racing, your stomach tightens, and maybe you even stop breathing for a moment. Your system has moved out of calm-and-connected (green zone) and into stressed-and-alert (yellow zone) because it senses something *might* be wrong.[6]

---

5. Joseph LeDoux, *The Emotional Brain: The Mysterious Underpinnings of Emotional Life* (Simon & Schuster, 1996).

6. Stephen W. Porges, *The Polyvagal Theory: Neurophysiological Foundations of Emotions, Attachment, Communication, and Self-Regulation* (W.W. Norton & Company, 2011).

2. Your brain adds a story (perception).

   o Once your body reacts, your brain runs in to make sense of it.[7] You're not just reading the email; you're filtering it through everything else—your physical sensations, like the tight chest or shallow breathing, and your past experiences, like that one time a client emailed something similar and it was bad news. Before you know it, your brain has pieced together a story: "They're upset with me" or "I must have done something wrong." Even though you haven't even opened the email, this combination of body signals and past experiences has you assuming the worst.[8]

At this point, things can go one of two ways. If you're feeling dysregulated, you might immediately fire off a response, trying to fix a problem that might not even exist—classic yellow-zone behavior. But if you practice the exercise that I share with you toward the end of this chapter, you'll pause, notice your body's stress signals, take a moment to regulate (you can use the Nervous System Cheat Sheet), and remind yourself: *I don't actually know what this email is about yet.* By grounding into curiosity, you rewrite the story: "This could be anything, and I'll respond when I'm ready." Now you're back in the green zone, able to handle the situation with clarity and confidence.

That's a taste of what's about to come, but before we can get to rewriting the stories, we need to know how to identify which nervous system stories come from dysregulation and therefore need your awareness to rewrite them. Take your time going slow with this—even if you want to rush ahead. No matter how much self-awareness you have, you always have

---

7. Bessel A. Van der Kolk, *The Body Keeps the Score: Brain, Mind, Body in the Healing of Trauma* (Viking, 2014).

8. Daniel J. *Siegel, The Developing Mind: How Relationships and the Brain Interact to Shape Who We Are,* 2nd ed. (Guilford Press, 2012).

dysregulated stories going on in the background. I've been practicing this for a decade and I literally just found a new one this morning waiting at a red traffic light.

Qualities of Dysregulated Nervous System Stories

Let's take a neutral example such as your colleague messaging to say they forgot to send you the full details of a project, and you now need to work on your day off to prepare for an event on Monday.

A fight response might say something like this:

"This is so unfair! I can't believe I have to sacrifice my day off because they messed up!"

"I'm not going to put up with this—I should tell them how irresponsible they are."

A flight response might say something like this:

"I should just ignore this and hope they don't expect much on Monday."

"Maybe I should find a different job where people respect my time better."

A fawn response might say something like this:

"Of course, I'll do it—no problem at all!" (even though it feels upsetting)

"I'll work extra hours over the weekend to make sure it's perfect, so they don't think I'm difficult."

A freeze response might say something like this:

Nothing! You feel paralyzed, overwhelmed by how unfair and exhausting this situation is, and struggle to make a decision.

"I don't even know where to start, and now the whole weekend feels ruined."

These dysregulated states have a few things in common:

They hyperfocus on threats.

When you're dysregulated, your brain presents you with more information about possible threats, feeding you anxious, fear-based thoughts. This is a primal response, designed to keep you safe if you're, say, being chased by a bear, but not exactly helpful when you're just trying to write a sales pitch or when your success relies on risk mitigation, not risk avoidance.

There is a negative bias.

A dysregulated nervous system amplifies negative thinking, so you're more likely to dwell on problems, anticipate worst-case scenarios, or fixate on setbacks. The amygdala, the brain's fear center, gets more active, making every situation feel way more difficult or dangerous than it actually is. Basically, you make it very hard for yourself to access the positive thinking, opportunistic thinking, and resiliency needed to find success in a difficult industry. On one hand you need to be aware of possible risks—but not at the expense of seeing possible opportunities.

They employ rigid, outdated thinking.

When you're dysregulated, the prefrontal cortex—responsible for things like decision-making and problem-solving—gets less active. Many founders I work with have relied on rigid thinking to succeed, but to reach the next level or adapt to industry changes, flexible thinking is essential—and it's easier to access in a regulated story.

Qualities of Regulated Nervous System Stories

When your nervous system is regulated, it means that your body and mind feel safe enough to connect with yourself and others and be creative, innovative, and positive. Here are some emotional qualities and assumptions about connection and oneself that are indicative of a regulated nervous system:

Emotional Qualities

- **Calmness**—a general sense of peace and relaxation. There's no urgency or anxiety, and you feel grounded in the present moment.
- **Empathy**—the ability to understand and share the feelings of others. You feel connected to others and can relate to their experiences with compassion.
- **Patience**—you have the capacity to wait without frustration. You tolerate delays or challenges without feeling overwhelmed.
- **Openness**—a willingness to be vulnerable and share your true self with others. You feel safe to express your thoughts and emotions without fear of judgment.
- **Confidence**—a belief in your abilities and self-worth. You trust in your capacity to handle situations as they arise.

- **Optimism**—a positive outlook on life and the future. You see challenges as opportunities for growth rather than insurmountable obstacles.
- **Resilience**—the ability to bounce back from setbacks. You can recover from stress or disappointment without getting stuck in negative emotions.
- **Gratitude**—a sense of appreciation for the positive aspects of your life. You focus on what you have rather than what you lack.

A regulated nervous system makes certain assumptions about life, and by identifying them now, it will become easier for you to write your regulated nervous system story.

Assumptions About Connection

- **People are trustworthy.** You assume that others have good intentions and can be trusted, unless proven otherwise.
- **Relationships are safe.** You believe that relationships are a source of support and comfort, and you feel safe to be yourself within them.
- **Connection is nurturing.** You view connection with others as a nourishing experience that enhances your well-being.
- **It's okay to rely on others.** You trust that you can lean on others for support when needed, and that they will be there for you.
- **Boundaries are respected.** You assume that others will respect your boundaries and that you can respect theirs without fear of losing the connection.
- **You are accepted.** You believe that you are accepted for who you are, flaws and all, and that you don't need to hide parts of yourself to be loved.

Assumptions About Yourself

- **I can trust myself.** You believe your inner voice is smart and a confident source of information. You believe that you can take on challenges and trust you can get through them and that you are good at making decisions.
- **I am worthy.** You believe that you are inherently valuable and deserving of love, respect, and good things in life.
- **I can handle challenges.** You trust in your ability to navigate difficulties and overcome obstacles.
- **I am capable.** You have confidence in your skills and abilities to achieve your goals.
- **I am lovable.** You believe that you are lovable just as you are, without needing to change or prove anything to anyone.
- **I deserve rest.** You understand the importance of rest and self-care, and you don't feel guilty for taking time for yourself.
- **I can make mistakes.** You accept that making mistakes is a part of being human, and you don't let them define your self-worth.
- **I have choices.** You believe that you have the power to make choices that align with your values and needs.
- **I belong.** You feel a sense of belonging in your relationships and communities, and you trust that you have a place in the world.

Going back to the example of a colleague messaging to say they forgot to send you the full project details and you now need to work on your day off, let's take a look at some regulated responses:

"I'm available for a couple of hours tomorrow but may need to prioritize key parts due to the short notice. Does that work for you?"

"It's not ideal, but I can make time on Sunday and set boundaries for future projects to avoid this."

"Thanks for letting me know. I won't be able to take on this work over the weekend, but I'm looking forward to the event and can catch up on details Monday morning to prepare. Let me know if there's anything specific you want me to focus on then!"

"I appreciate you reaching out, and I understand things can slip through the cracks. I won't be able to cover this on my day off, but I'm excited to dive in on Monday. Please let me know any high-priority items for then, and we'll make it a great event!"

The key to these responses is that they are genuine. When saying them, you're filled with a sense of compassion, courage, excitement, understanding, and ease.

Accessing the nervous system story is a skill anyone can learn, and this exercise will help you do so.

EXERCISE: Find Your Regulated Nervous System Story

Step 1: Notice activation.

- Check in with your body. Begin by tuning in to your physical sensations, emotions, and thoughts. Pay attention to signs of nervous system activation such as increased heart rate, shallow breathing, muscle tension, or feelings of anxiety.
- Identify the trigger. Reflect on what might have triggered this response. Was it an external event, a thought, or an internal sensation?

Example: You receive an email asking for an urgent change to a piece of work you've already completed. You notice that your heart rate increases, and your mind starts racing.

Step 2: Write down your initial perception.

- Capture the narrative by writing down what you're currently thinking and feeling. Describe how you are perceiving the situation and connect it to a nervous system state. You can reference chapters 1 and 4 to refresh your memory on nervous system states if needed.
- Note and acknowledge any physical sensations you're experiencing.

Examples:

A fight response would be "I feel angry because this request is unfair and last-minute. My thoughts are focused on how unappreciated I feel. My chest feels tight, and I have an urge to write a defensive reply."

A flight response would be "I feel panicked and want to avoid dealing with this. My thoughts are centered on escaping the situation—maybe I can ignore the email or pretend I didn't see it. My hands are shaking, and I'm feeling a strong urge to step away from my computer."

A fawn response would be "I feel anxious and immediately want to please the person who sent the email. My thoughts are about how I can make them happy, even if it means staying up all night to make the changes. My stomach feels knotted, and I feel an urge to respond immediately with an apology and a promise to fix everything."

A freeze response would be "I feel overwhelmed and stuck. My thoughts are jumbled, and I can't think clearly about what to do next. My body feels heavy, and I find it hard to move or make a decision. I just want to sit here, doing nothing."

Step 3: Write the regulated nervous system story.

Using the information in this chapter on regulated nervous system stories, pick one assumption about yourself or others that resonates with you or feels challenging for you and practice writing a story about the scenario you're contemplating from this place.

If I assume [enter assumption from above], how would I interpret this event?

Examples:

"This request is not a personal attack. The person might be under pressure themselves, and I can choose to respond calmly, setting boundaries if needed."

"Avoiding the email won't solve the problem. I can take a moment to assess what's being asked and respond in a way that is manageable for me."

"I see that I don't have to overextend myself to make this person happy. I can offer a reasonable solution without compromising my own well-being."

"Even though it doesn't feel like it, I am capable of taking action. I can break down the task into smaller steps and start with one small action, like drafting a response to the email."

Step 4: Pick the empowering story.

- Compare the two narratives, and look at the differences between your initial and revised narratives. Identify the nervous system story that was initially shaping your perception.
- Understand the root. Put a pin in this experience and return to it in pillar 2 where you'll learn about what underlying belief or past experience might have contributed to this nervous system story.

Step 5: Challenge the original nervous system story.

- Question the validity of your nervous system. Ask yourself "Is this story absolutely true? What evidence do I have for and against it?"
- Move closer to your regulated nervous system story. Consider other possible interpretations of the situation.

Examples:

A fight response would be "Is it true that I'm being attacked? Or could it be that the person is just stressed and needs help?"

A flight response would be "Is it true that I can't handle this? Or could I take one small step that would make the task more manageable?"

A fawn response would be "Is it true that I have to do everything perfectly to be valued? Or could I set boundaries and still be respected?"

A freeze response would be "Is it true that I'm powerless? Or could I take one small action that would help me move forward?"

I recommend practicing this exercise daily for twenty-eight days to help train yourself to recognize and choose the regulated story more often.

Setting aside a specific time on your calendar is essential to ensure you have the space to build this habit.

Debbie skipped scheduling time, thinking she'd develop the habit naturally. This is a common approach—many people assume they'll be able to incorporate it automatically. While that may work for a few, most of us need a bit more structure. Rewiring patterns in the brain and nervous system requires consistency and dedicated practice. Because she didn't make a conscious effort to observe her nervous system stories, Debbie found it hard to step back from her thoughts and ended up believing her dysregulated stories as truth. Three specific thoughts held her back:

- Belinda had called the quiz pseudoscience, making Debbie feel she was silly to trust her own instincts.
- She'd read that successful people are positive and resilient, so she kept beating herself up for not being more positive, which clouded her thinking.
- She fixated on the belief that she'd never know enough to be paid better.

Because Debbie couldn't shift to a regulated nervous system story, her dysregulation deepened, and things began to unravel quickly. Her stomach issues escalated into full-blown IBS, leaving her in constant pain and dealing with unpredictable bathroom trips. At home, she felt her partner pulling away, their conversations growing tense and distant, and her child's principal called, voicing concerns about disruptive behavior at school. Debbie felt paralyzed, unsure how to fix any of it. Tasks and to-dos piled up, each one feeling heavier than the last, and her mind was barely managing the constant decisions and mental load. The recent client complaint still gnawed at her confidence, amplifying a spiral of shame and negativity. Overwhelmed and on the edge, she had an idea: get a virtual assistant.

Emily found it hard to stick to her twenty-eight-day commitment but decided to keep practicing by using her attitude of progress and learning over perfection. Now that Emily knew her thoughts were the result of a perceived threat around the uncertainty and newness of this new venture, and they weren't actually true, she could separate herself from them and focus enough to create a new sales and marketing strategy that was very effective—immediately.

While it felt like things couldn't possibly get better, somehow, they did. Emily expected nothing more than a simple dinner when her partner invited her out. The evening was peaceful, almost predictable, until they strolled home under the stars and took an unexpected detour through the park where they'd had their first date. Every visit to this spot made her heart skip a beat, but tonight was different. As they walked, tiny lights began to twinkle in the trees, casting a soft, magical glow, turning their familiar path into something out of a dream.

When they reached the bench where they'd once shared their quiet hopes for the future, her partner suddenly dropped to one knee, stumbling slightly in excitement. Emily's heart raced, her breath catching as the reality of the moment dawned on her. And then came the words she'd secretly been waiting to hear: "Will you marry me?" Warmth rushed through her, her chest tightened with joy and disbelief, her eyes brimmed with tears. She managed one word, a joyful, breathless "Yes!" as she threw her arms around him, overwhelmed by happiness.

That single, perfect moment shattered the walls she'd unknowingly built around her life, filling every part of it with ease and lightness. Joy began to spill into every corner of her world, creating a profound sense of emotional freedom she hadn't known was possible. The weight she'd carried for years lifted; she felt a freedom she'd never imagined was possible. She felt vibrantly alive for the first time in ages, and in this new atmosphere of joy, her child began thriving at school. At work, everything began clicking into place even more, and Emily knew she was ready to grow her team.

Key Takeaways

- Nervous system stories are narratives your brain constructs based on physiological signals, influenced by past experiences and your environment, that impact how you interpret reality, especially under stress.
- Stress triggers physiological changes, like increased cortisol, that shape thought patterns. This leads to hyperfocusing on threats, negative bias, and impaired cognitive flexibility, distorting your perception of reality.
- By noticing physical sensations and reflecting on them, you can challenge your initial stress-driven narrative, replacing it with a balanced, compassionate perspective, promoting healthier emotional and cognitive responses.

Now that you've identified your nervous system stories, I recommend practicing this daily for twenty-eight days. This consistent effort will help you naturally shift to finding your more regulated story and, over time, it'll become second nature! As you keep building this habit, you're ready to dive into pillar 2 of the BBB methodology, where you'll accomplish the following:

1. Reduce the strain on your mind and body from chronic stress.
2. Create the space needed to address the deeper root causes of your dysregulation, so that you can spend less energy regulating and more on building an impactful, purpose-driven business—all without compromising your health, values, or well-being.

Pillar 2: Trauma Healing

It's hard to write about trauma, and I've rewritten this particular part about thirteen different times. Every time I come to it, I feel a pull in my heart. There are parts of me that want *trauma* to be a word we utter, softly, only in moments we can appreciate the heaviness and pain that it carries in the hearts of us all. One that your body can never forget. Once you know this level of pain, you're forever joined with all the other humans who see this pain too. You communicate with each other in funny little nods—"I get it"—and deep sighs.

On the other side of that coin, I want us to speckle the word *trauma* around in our days, recognizing that we are all experiences of trauma—past, current, and future—and it is just another aspect of humanness we all navigate together. Trauma is a thread of the tapestry that connects us all.

And yet, it's highly individual. As Dr. Gabor Maté said, "Trauma is not what happens to you. Trauma is what happens inside you as a result of what happens to you."[9]

---

9. *The wisdom of trauma*, directed by Zaya Benazzo and Maurizio Benazzo (Science and Nonduality, 2021).

In the coming chapters, you will learn how to do the following:

- Understand what trauma is and how it affects how you perceive life, business, and success.
- Connect to the deepest essence of who you are—someone who feels deeply enough, supported, calm, and at ease.
- Create an action plan to combat common barriers to trauma healing.
- Process your emotions so that you can access more resilience and somatic intelligence.
- Find more empowering beliefs.
- And finally, expand your nervous system capacity for success.

Chapter 6

You Can't Heal Without the Self

Debbie had promised to be ready by 6:00 p.m. But now, at 6:15, she was still glued to her laptop, fingers racing over the keyboard, her gaze locked on the screen. A glass of red wine sat untouched beside her, holding deep reflections of the warm light overhead. She was laser-focused on perfecting onboarding documents for her new virtual assistant—who she'd spend the last of her savings employing. Her body filled with tension as she clenched her jaw, determined not to make a single mistake.

Her partner, Alex, walked over with dinner plates in hand, their initial excitement for a cozy Tuesday night together visibly dimmed. They hovered nearby, offering a strained smile. "Honey, are you ready?" they asked, the words edged with disappointment. What was meant to be a quiet evening had, once again, been eclipsed by Debbie's work. Barely looking up, Debbie replied, "Yep! Let's start eating—I just need to finish this while we go. It won't take long." She was so engrossed that she missed the hurt in Alex's eyes. Her world had shrunk to the size of her laptop screen, and the drive to keep pushing forward blinded her to the life slipping away around her, moment by missed moment.

Across town, Emily was also entrenched in her hiring process. Though she'd enjoyed a recent boost in revenue, the thrill of success was beginning to fade. No matter how much she rested, a deep fatigue clung to her, and an underlying sense of dread loomed. *Start-ups fail every day! This is a battle—we have to work harder, be better!* her inner voice insisted, leaving her frazzled and unfocused. Small mistakes began to slip in—typos, billing errors—each one subtly eroding her clients' trust. Logically, she knew her business was stable, but her nervous system was on high alert, bracing for an invisible blow.

Neither Debbie nor Emily realized how much past pain, fear, and trauma were steering their thoughts, emotions, and actions. They were caught in a painful cycle of ambition and survival, unable to see it clearly, much less break free.

It made perfect sense—it happens to us all. Trauma often resurfaces in entrepreneurship, where constant uncertainty and challenging growth can push old wounds to the surface. This can limit our access to the creativity, innovation, and sustainable ways of working that allow us to make a meaningful impact in the world, earn a profit, and still preserve our individual and collective well-being.

When Debbie and Emily sat down for their next session, I could sense their apprehension, a scattered energy buzzing between them. Taking a few grounding breaths, I used my mind to direct those breaths to my lower back (a grounding technique useful when your nervous system is a little activated), preparing myself to hold space for what might be a deep, possibly painful session. I began to explain that by unburdening the nervous system from trauma and unhealthy coping mechanisms, we can reclaim our natural creativity, resilience, and capacity for success. This work allows us to return to our true essence—our authentic Self.

Your Self is your access to trauma healing that works long-term and feels as easy as it can. No matter how hard you try, there's no effective or easeful way to do trauma healing or personal development, or to create success that feels aligned with your values and health without establishing and consistently returning to this foundation of Self.

So what is the Self? The Self isn't something that you "do" or a part of you. It's the core of who you are, and a way you practice "being." It's that innate, undamaged, wise center that is grounded, calm, compassionate, creative, and curious.

This BBB session—and therefore this chapter—was focused on creating a strong foundation of Self, so that when we dive deeper to examine some of the pain, discomfort, or unhealthy coping mechanisms you may be experiencing, we're approaching it from a place where genuine change and healing can occur. When we operate from a place of Self, we have the patience needed to handle the uncertainties, ups and downs, and questions that arise. We approach the work with love and care for ourselves, not from a desire to "fix" or reinforce that something is wrong.

Taking the time to ground in the foundation of Self will allow your nervous system to find the safety it needs to release the protective patterns it holds. By operating from a place of ease and accessing your somatic intelligence, you'll make better decisions, connect more deeply with others, and create a meaningful impact in the world.

EXERCISE: Coming Home to the Self

This exercise is designed to create a secure foundation for trauma healing. I will guide you in connecting to your core—your Self—and help you identify ways to proactively connect with your Self over the next few weeks, so you can cultivate the strength, compassion, curiosity, and nervous system capacity needed for trauma healing. It's essential that you regularly take time to connect with your Self.

In the upcoming chapters, we will process emotions, revisit past traumatic experiences, and work on helping parts of ourselves relax, releasing protective mechanisms and unproductive coping patterns. Your connection to Self will directly influence how much success, clarity, and ease you experience as you engage with these exercises, ultimately supporting your ability to create sustainable success in life and business through your somatic intelligence.

Below you will find a list of qualities that represent aspects of the Self. As you read through, take your time to explore each quality as a felt sense in your body—that's your pathway to your Self.

Step 1: Read slowly. Take a deep breath as you read each quality, allowing yourself to fully receive it. Notice how your breath, any sensations you're having, and even your thoughts may shift as you connect with each word. There will be some words that evoke a feeling of resonance or connection inside of you, similar to when you're plucking strings on a guitar and you hit the right chord and feel a vibration. The words that evoke that feeling inside of you are the words you can use as your connection to Self. There will be other words that don't evoke anything—you can ignore those words.

Step 2: Ask questions. Get curious about each quality by asking yourself questions without any pressure to find specific answers:

- What does this quality feel like in my body?
- What sensations or imagery does it evoke? A color, a shape, a breath pattern?
- Is there a scent, memory, or symbol it brings to mind?

Step 3: Explore and make it your own. When there are words you don't resonate with, explore similar words that do resonate. You can do this by looking at synonyms or looking at the meaning of the word and finding a word that has a similar essence that feels more true for you. For example, you may not resonate with *purity*, but you do resonate with *clarity*, and from your perspective, this feels similar and interchangeable.

Note: It is normal and natural to experience some resistance to these words and qualities. This might look like trying to rush through the list, holding your breath, feeling tension inside, becoming distracted, judging the words, or rolling your eyes. This is a practice that can take some time to make sense of, so take your time as you move through it, and if it doesn't make sense straight away, that's okay—keep trying.

The Qualities of the Self

- **Being-ness**—a state of simply being, not doing.
- **Harmony**—the ability to hold all parts of yourself with peace.
- **Purity**—feeling deeply connected to yourself, free from outside influences.
- **Constructive**—focused on building and uplifting yourself and others.
- **Virtuous**—guided by uplifting values and morals.

- **Consciousness and presence**—self-awareness and a connection to the present moment.
- **Compassion**—extending empathy and kindness to yourself and others.
- **Confidence**—self-assurance and trust in yourself.
- **Creativity**—generating new ideas and solutions.
- **Connectedness**—recognizing your connection to all beings and the universe.

- **Serenity and calmness**—finding peace, even in chaos.
- **Steadiness and clarity**—a calm joy and a clear, broad view of any situation.
- **Embodiment**—being aware and present in your body.
- **Curiosity**—a readiness for new experiences and learning.
- **Perspective**—seeing things from multiple angles.
- **Purpose**—having direction and meaning in life.
- **Power**—the ability to create change in your environment.
- **Possibility**—openness to new experiences and growth.
- **Relaxed muscles and deep breath**—a natural state of ease.

Now that you're familiar with these qualities, how can you bring them into your life more often?

- Can you evoke them from within regularly? If so, try practicing this a few times a day.
- Are there certain practices, rituals, or activities that bring these experiences out in you? People often find that playing cards, doing breathwork, walking, or writing helps them connect with these qualities. Notice what works for you, and make a strong, conscious effort to engage in these activities regularly, preferably every day, even in small ways.

If you resonate with a word that you don't know how to connect with every day, that's fine—you can explore and experiment! For example, if you want to resonate more deeply with *purpose*, you can start exploring and learning about what that means to you, via learning what it means to other people. As you are learning and researching, keep coming back to another anchor of Self (pick one of the other words). One day, you'll feel a resonance or "click" in your body that will tell you what purpose means for you, and you'll have another pathway to Self.

To complete this exercise, try to walk away with a word or experience you *do* feel you can access fairly easily—that will be your pathway to Self. It might be *curiosity*, and you can be curious about things. Perhaps, it's *possibility*, and you can allow your mind to daydream about possibilities a few times a week. Or it might be the relaxed muscles that you feel after a boxing class, and you can do more boxing classes or other activities that get you in a state of physical relaxation.

I recommend returning to this practice multiple times a day to deepen your familiarity with your Self. This will help you create the nervous system wiring and the patterns that support healing trauma, accessing somatic intelligence, and finding success.

As Debbie read through the list, she felt *power*, *perspective*, and *compassion* centered in her belly, a warm, golden color radiating from within. Later, while washing dishes, she found herself in a big argument with Alex over a trivial issue—how the mop was stored in the laundry. The warm water ran over her hands, and the sound of clinking dishes echoed as she felt a surge of frustration. Thankfully, her mind drifted to her session, and she remembered her Self—the part of her capable of experiencing the disagreement without becoming overwhelmed. She visualized that bright golden light rising from her belly to her heart, connecting her back to her center.

Things began to feel a bit lighter. Although she couldn't fully reconnect with Alex that evening, she did notice a deeper sense of grounding and hope. That night, she slept through peacefully and woke up with renewed energy, even skipping her morning coffee. Over the following weeks, however, her business—once a domain she felt in control of—began to slip. Her new VA was barely meeting expectations, forcing Debbie to catch errors and redo tasks, her workload growing every single day. Gradually, the vision she held for her business seemed to fade under the weight of mounting stress. She felt as if she were sinking in quicksand, each effort to regain control only dragging her down further. Yet she continued to connect to that golden light within, feeling more aligned with her Self and eager for the next BBB session, hoping to learn how to lift the heaviness she was carrying.

Emily, on the other hand, felt her connection to Self as something soft, slow, and graceful, resonating most with the qualities of peace and clarity. Reflecting on times when she'd felt this way, she realized she often experienced it when taking her time to drink a cup of tea. She decided to introduce a similar ritual into her afternoon routine, creating a peaceful tea moment between 3:00 and 3:15. As she sipped her green tea, feeling the warmth flow down her throat, she took a few deep breaths, closing her eyes as calm settled over her. For those fifteen minutes, she practiced being peaceful and looking at where in her life she felt clarity so that she could bring more of it into her work projects and interactions for the rest of the day.

Over the weeks, her fatigue lifted, replaced by a calm, steady energy that felt sustainable. Her mistakes dwindled, and when they did occur, she approached them with ease, avoiding any spiral of self-doubt. Clients noticed the shift, drawn to the authenticity and grounded clarity she now exuded. One even commented, "You seem so grounded. Working with you feels different lately."

At home, Emily's new presence made it easier for her child to open up. They shared deeper conversations over dinner, with her child confiding about friendships and school worries. Emily's connection to her Self allowed her to offer gentle encouragement without rushing to fix things, deepening their bond with trust and warmth.

Key Takeaways

- Establishing a strong connection to the Self—the calm, wise, and undamaged core within you—creates a solid foundation for trauma healing, fostering easeful and lasting transformation.
- The Self embodies qualities like compassion, creativity, curiosity, and steadiness, allowing you to approach challenges with patience and love, rather than from a place of needing to "fix" yourself.
- Regularly connecting with the Self, whether through visualizations, mindfulness, or intentional activities, helps your nervous system release protective patterns and access resilience, clarity, and deeper connections with others.

Now that you have found a pathway to your Self and set up a regular practice, you're ready to identify, bring awareness to, and validate your past traumatic experiences.

Chapter 7

Your Pain Is Valid

Debbie was overly meticulous with her new VA, reviewing every small detail, double-checking tasks, and repeatedly following up on items even after she'd delegated them. She felt compelled to micromanage, unable to fully trust her VA to handle tasks independently, despite knowing this was slowing down her own productivity.

Emily, on the other hand, found herself caught in a cycle of hesitation and second-guessing. She kept rethinking instructions before sending them to her assistant, often revising tasks multiple times before delegating. She hesitated to ask for support on larger projects, worried that her assistant might see her as unqualified if she didn't handle everything perfectly. Her struggle to relax showed in her constant attempts to appear competent, even at the cost of overloading herself with tasks she could have let go, leaving her drained and unfocused.

What neither woman could see was that these struggles were stemming from past traumatic experiences. For Debbie, her tight grip on control pointed to a fear of letting go, as if any mistake or misstep might lead to catastrophe. This traced back to a traumatic experience from her past, when she had trusted someone deeply only to be betrayed, leaving her in profound pain. For Emily, her need to handle everything herself and appear exceptionally competent stemmed from her father's consistent questioning of her intelligence as she grew up. Her business had become an unconscious way to prove her worth and intelligence.

How Trauma Is Created in the Nervous System

We know that the nervous system is a network of cells and fibers running throughout the body to help us understand, respond to, and integrate information from both our environment and inner experiences—this process is known as neuroception. It continuously assesses our surroundings and our internal states to gauge safety and determine how to respond. Depending on what it perceives, the nervous system prompts us to engage socially, fight, flee, appease, or freeze. This response impacts our muscles, digestion, breathing, heart rate, and other bodily functions, as well as the thoughts and emotions that enter our awareness to keep us safe.

Importantly, all of this communication happens autonomously; we never need to consciously direct it. Through this system, we digest experiences, allowing us to process them fully without lingering painful emotions, beliefs, or perceptions. However, trauma occurs when our body cannot fully digest an experience, return to a sense of safety, and learn from it. Trauma sets off a cascade of physiological, psychological, and neurological changes that affect physical, emotional, mental, and even spiritual well-being, often limiting our ability to make grounded, life-affirming choices.

When trauma overwhelms the nervous system beyond its ability to process an experience, it shuts down the prefrontal cortex—the brain region responsible for complex cognitive functions, such as decision-making, emotional regulation, attention, working memory, and problem-solving. This shutdown leaves a lasting imprint on the psyche. With this primal response triggered, the body not only has to work through the physical stress response but also adopts new, often painful, perceptions of the world. These altered understandings feel so threatening and distressing that the mind, body, and emotional systems reconfigure to manage and cope with the lasting impact.

Trauma is created when we are unable to digest (process and assimilate fully) an experience in the moment. A well-digested experience (like a satiating and well-digested meal) enriches and enlivens you. It nourishes the mind and spirit, fostering clarity, resilience, and a sense of inner harmony. You can think of it as the last overwhelmingly beautiful experience you had. Maybe you got a bit emotional, but you walked away from the experience feeling supported by your community, and loved, and you learned some lessons. You might even have forgotten about it now, meaning it was well digested.

Just as with food, when an experience is not fully digested—meaning it is not fully processed or integrated—it can lead to imbalance, stagnation, or stress within the body and mind. To effectively digest an experience in the moment means the experience doesn't leave residual pain, fear, disempowering beliefs, or stagnant energy in the body or mind. Unfortunately, there are many painful things in our life that happen that we don't have the ability to digest either because we don't have the support, skills or life experience, or because they are simply wrong, inhumane, and we should not ever get used to digesting them—they shouldn't be happening.

When you experience trauma, as the experience occurs the thoughts, emotions, and sensations it creates in the body are too much to process and assimilate so instead, the experience is stored by your nervous system as something to digest later and when you then have more capacity (i.e., space, skills, support, or safety). Oftentimes, when your body feels you have those things, it will present sensations, emotions, thoughts, and feelings into your reality to digest (experience)—even if that's very inconvenient

Trauma leaves a deep imprint. Trauma impacts the core of your being, affecting how you perceive and experience life from a soul, heart, and psyche level. If left stored in your system, it can create patterns of protection that come from pain and fear, and create more pain and fear in your life (such as how Debbie's fear of failure is creating pain in her relationship because she can't be present for her partner). This layer of trauma can be addressed through parts work, which I'll introduce shortly.

When I say that entrepreneurship can trigger trauma, I'm referring to the way present-day experiences can activate your nervous system in a similar way to past traumatic events. It's as though your nervous system has a memory bank of intense or stressful experiences. When something in your current environment resembles or reminds you of a past trauma—maybe a certain way someone said something, a sound, a situation, or even a particular feeling—your nervous system can respond as if that old threat is happening all over again. This can lead to physical sensations (like a racing heart, sweating, or an urge to complete a task), emotions (such as fear or anxiety), and thoughts (like *something will go wrong* or *I can't handle this*) that mirror the original traumatic event.

In essence, the nervous system becomes triggered because it's been conditioned to react to certain cues, believing it needs to protect you even when the current situation isn't genuinely threatening. Something that's always amazed and reassured me is that our nervous system isn't only shaped by our personal experiences but can also carry responses from past generations. Studies suggest that the nervous system interprets its current reality—and what it deems necessary for safety, survival, and thriving—

based on ancestral experiences passed down through genetic memory.[10] An interesting example comes from research conducted at Emory University. In this study, mice were conditioned to associate the scent of a cherry smell with a mild electric shock. Surprisingly, the offspring of these mice, without any exposure to the shock, displayed heightened sensitivity and fear toward the same scent, demonstrating to us how fear responses can be inherited across generations.

This fear response wasn't limited to the immediate offspring but also appeared in the subsequent generation, suggesting that trauma or learned behavior was inherited through epigenetic mechanisms, environmental factors, such as trauma or stress, that influence traits that can be inherited by future generations. This highlights how traumatic experiences can create effects that reach beyond individual lifetimes, influencing future generations.[11]

Considering that our ancestral nervous systems shape how we interpret the world, and that even in recent history, events like slavery, the Holocaust, colonialism, apartheid, modern-day genocides, political unrest, and the struggles of various feminist movements taught women and minorities that success, visibility in leadership, or financial power could be dangerous, it's clear why we might unconsciously hold back from the extraordinary lives we consciously desire. Our nervous systems may be operating on the belief that standing out equates to a risk to our safety.

10 Rachel Yehuda and Amy Lehrner, "Intergenerational transmission of trauma effects: putative role of epigenetic mechanisms," *World Psychiatry 17*, no. 3 (2018): 243–257, https://doi.org/10.1002/wps.20568; Rebecca S. Moore, Rachel Kaletsky, and Coleen T. Murphy, "Piwi/PRG-1 Argonaute and TGF-β Mediate Transgenerational Learned Pathogenic Avoidance," *Cell 177*, no. 7 (2019): 1827–1841, https://doi.org/10.1016/j.cell.2019.05.024.

11. Quinn Eastman, "Mice can inherit learned sensitivity to a smell," Emory News Center, Emory University, news.emory.edu, December 2, 2013, https://news.emory.edu/stories/2013/12/smell_epigenetics_ressler/campus.html.

The lessons our nervous systems absorbed during those challenging times—both our own and those of our ancestors—were essential for survival then, but they aren't particularly helpful when we're trying to stand out and make our unique marketing or business ideas thrive.

As you navigate your journey as a leader, visionary, entrepreneur, or founder, understanding how your nervous system experiences life—and how trauma may shape those experiences—can be incredibly valuable. This perspective gives your logical mind a grounding point, helping you make sense of the challenges that arise as you build your business.

When I introduced this exercise to Debbie and Emily, it was like a light switched on for them—everything began to make sense. They felt a surge of self-compassion, let go of the feeling that something was inherently wrong with them, and gained clarity on where to focus to feel better and move forward with greater confidence in building their business.

EXERCISE: Identifying How Your Trauma Influences Your Success and Ease

Here are some key points to keep in mind:

- This exercise isn't a cognitive heavy thinking exercise. Meaning the questions below aren't journal prompts I want you to answer with a few bullet points, but rather a contemplation I invite you to allow to float around in your mind until the answers appear. This could take thirty seconds, days, months, or years. There is enough space and time to let them appear when necessary.
- Remember that trauma is the internal effect of the event, not the event itself. What was traumatic for me might be neutral for you, and what is neutral for me might be traumatic for you. If

you experience a situation as a threat to your safety or existence (actual or presumed) to the extent that your nervous system goes into extreme dysregulation and self-preservation, that event will remain traumatic for you. This counts for moments you didn't think you were dysregulated in, or protecting yourself from at the time.

- The more sensitive you are, the more you feel and the less it takes to hurt you, particularly in comparison to people who are less sensitive and more stoic. Very sensitive people (like myself) experience things deeply, both pain and, when feeling safe, pleasure.

- Trauma is not synonymous with suffering nor bad things happening to people. Life is suffering. Suffering is pain. However, pain only becomes traumatic when it does not have the support it needs to be digested and integrated into growth.

Here's a self-reflective exercise to try:

- Our nervous system learns through things we experience ourselves (such as going through a divorce) and what other people experience (such as seeing most of your friends' parents experience divorce or your best friend experience divorce). Keeping that in mind, what experiences in life that you have been a part of, or witnessed, have left you feeling unsafe and untrusting of others?

- Have there been moments it's felt like you've gone into "protect yourself" mode and lacked access to the wise, playful, creative, and analytical thinking part of your mind and body?

- As you read through the following traumatic events, contemplate the question "What might have been traumatic for my system?"

- Consider how this may be influencing how you engage with your business, your sales, your community, and your work. Some common observations will be listed below to help you self-identify.

Instructions

Circle each of the events that may have affected you or your ancestors. Keep in mind that the items listed here are examples to represent many experiences, and your experiences might vary significantly.

1. Interpersonal trauma

- Having a sense of tension in the house
- Being unsure if your needs will be met by a caregiver
- Physical abuse
- Sexual abuse or assault
- Emotional or psychological abuse (including ongoing gaslighting, betrayal, and neglect)
- Domestic violence
- Bullying or harassment

If you have a history of interpersonal trauma (which most, if not all, adults do), you may struggle with trust, leading to difficulties in building and maintaining healthy business relationships. You might experience heightened anxiety in situations that require vulnerability, such as networking, pitching to investors, or negotiating contracts. This could manifest as avoiding delegating tasks due to a lack of trust in others, leading to burnout and inefficiency.

2. Loss and grief

- Death of a loved one
- Miscarriage or stillbirth
- Separation or divorce
- Loss of a job or significant life change

The loss of a loved one or a significant life change (such as your parents' divorce) can result in profound grief that affects focus, motivation, and overall well-being. This may become ingrained as a feeling that good things end, resulting in you always preparing for the worst-case scenario.

While planning for the worst-case scenario can be helpful in some situations, utilizing your mental energy this way can prevent you from seeing new opportunities present today. Additionally, this feeling is a sign that your body is in a prolonged stress response (it perceives danger—an assumed loss in the future), which can create long-term health concerns. Because your body's energy is in protect mode, it makes decision-making and engaging with clients *so much harder* than it needs to be, simply because your body thinks they are a threat to your safety when, actually, they are the doorway to your ease and the achievement of your purpose.

3. Accidents and injuries

- Car accidents
- Workplace accidents
- Sports injuries
- Natural disasters (e.g., earthquakes, floods)

If you've experienced serious accidents or injuries, you might live with chronic pain, physical limitations, or lack of energy. You may have difficulty concentrating and have a hard time performing daily tasks. While you're probably still carrying some (very fair!) frustration with you, you might also be feeling a sense of helplessness, or your nervous system has learned that you are helpless or unable to do something, simply because that has either been objectively true in the past or perceived to be true.

Perceived or real helplessness is one of the most dysregulating states your nervous system can experience, leaving your body feeling like it's in imminent danger with no way out—it truly feels like a matter of life and death. This can manifest in various ways, from feeling significant concern about financial instability (no matter the amount of money in your bank account), to feeling overwhelmed by workloads your colleagues seem to manage with grace and ease, or feeling paralyzed at the idea that you might be rejected. You might also find yourself repeatedly seeking help for the same problem or feeling like life is unfair.

Physically, this often feels like tightness in the chest, fatigue, or restlessness, while thoughts like *I can't do this* or *Life is stacked against me* run through your mind. Emotionally, you may feel anxious, frustrated, or hopeless, leading to actions like procrastination, overworking, or withdrawing from crucial opportunities. While helplessness is a challenging state to escape, it can be done with the right strategies, which we'll explore below.

4. Medical trauma

- Illnesses or medical conditions
- Birth trauma
- Invasive medical procedures or surgeries
- Chronic pain or debilitating health issues
- Life-threatening or near-death experiences

If you have a history of medical trauma, such as serious illnesses or invasive procedures, you may experience ongoing fear about your health, leading to anxiety or depression. You may have also a belief that people won't listen to you, or that you do not have choices or the ability to create the change you want in the world. During your trauma, this was likely true, as your body or people you trusted created scenarios and experiences that you did not want to experience. This can manifest as a fear of taking risks, difficulty planning for the future, or an inability to fully engage with your business due to preoccupation with health concerns.

If you've experienced medical trauma, you might hesitate to start or expand your business, fearing the physical and emotional toll that increased responsibilities could bring or thinking that you won't be able to achieve it. On the flip side, you might become reckless and push yourself to burnout and overwhelm trying to achieve all you can, as quickly as you can, in an effort to feel seen and heard (to make up for when you weren't) or to make sense of, or escape, the sad reality that life can be very unfair and hard, and one day it will end.

5. Combat and war

- Military combat experiences
- Exposure to war zones and violence
- Post-traumatic stress among veterans

If you've experienced either firsthand or secondhand combat or war, you might experience some symptoms of PTSD or complex PTSD. This includes being in combat or having combat in your hometown, but it also can mean growing up in countries with civil unrest and instability, either from your personal experience or that of your ancestors. These symptoms might often look like hypervigilance, difficulty focusing, and challenges with emotional regulation. They can make it hard to navigate the unpredictable nature of entrepreneurship, where stress and uncertainty are common.

Hypervigilance, emotional dysregulation, and difficulty with concentration can manifest as constant anxiety about potential business failures, avoidance of certain situations, intense emotional reactions to setbacks, and struggles with maintaining focus on tasks or projects. Long term, this can lead to burnout, procrastination, and inconsistent business performance due to the overwhelming stress and mental fatigue.

6. Childhood trauma

- Neglect or abandonment
- Physical, emotional, or sexual abuse
- Witnessing domestic violence or substance abuse
- Divorce or parental separation

Childhood trauma, such as neglect or abuse, can create deep-seated beliefs of unworthiness or fear of failure. This can lead to self-sabotage, perfectionism, or an inability to take constructive criticism, all of which can hinder business growth and personal development.

This is a big topic, and I could never cover it in a few sentences. In fact, it's what most of this book is dedicated to understanding from different perspectives. Inside of every entrepreneur I've ever worked with or witnessed, there is, without a doubt, a part of themselves choosing entrepreneurship and their specific path in an attempt to heal their childhood trauma while also being impacted and limited by it.

Oprah Winfrey became the most influential Black woman in America, fueled by her need to make other people feel seen, heard, and valued—something she rarely experienced as a child.[12] Another example is how Jenny at my local coworking space wants to create communities for women who feel alone because she's felt alone since she was a young child. It also looks like how my client Jessica struggles with sales conversations and

---

12. Bruce D. Perry and Oprah Winfrey, *What Happened to You? Conversations on Trauma, Resilience, and Healing* (Flatiron Books, 2021).

"doesn't want to be salesy" because she's nervous it will come across as manipulative, and her mother has been hurting her through manipulation since she was young.

7. Displacement and migration

- Refugee experiences
- Forced migration
- Displacement due to conflict, financial hardship, or disaster

If you've experienced forced migration or displacement, you might carry a sense of instability and fear of loss, affecting your ability to take risks or to trust in long-term business planning. You may also struggle with feelings of alienation or not belonging, which can impact your confidence and networking abilities.

A refugee entrepreneur might hesitate to invest in their business or form long-term partnerships, fearing that their success could be easily taken away or disrupted by external circumstances. You may find it hard to even believe that what you want is possible, and because you're living with the idea that what you want isn't possible, what's the point in trying? This can feel like a big tug-of-war inside of you and may appear as erratic behavior, such as going all in on your mission for a few months then, when you start seeing success, feeling like you need to pull back and relax, costing you the momentum you were starting to build.

8. Community trauma

- Acts of terrorism
- Mass shootings
- Natural disasters affecting a community
- Collective violence or unrest

Experiencing or witnessing community trauma, such as acts of terrorism or natural disasters, can lead to collective fear and a sense of helplessness. You might find it difficult to stay motivated or optimistic about your business, especially if the trauma has led to economic downturns or social unrest.

When thinking about the future, you might feel overwhelmed by the magnitude of the challenges ahead and experience helplessness (feeling like there's no point), focus excessively on short-term pleasure and gain, and either completely avoid long-term planning or struggle with it. On the contrary, you might feel a deep pull to help others, fueled by the unconscious belief (that is sometimes true) that if you don't help, no one will. In the same way that you may have chosen entrepreneurship to try and help your past self or your community, you might find yourself drawn to entrepreneurial ventures that create social impact as a way of healing your own community trauma.

9. Systemic trauma

- Oppression
- Bullying
- Prejudice
- Discrimination
- Hate crimes and exploitation (e.g., colonization, internment camps, slavery, the Holocaust, post-migration discrimination and mistreatment)
- Discrimination and judgment based on gender or sexual orientation

If you have faced systemic trauma, you might carry internalized beliefs of inferiority or fear of further marginalization. This can limit your willingness to step into leadership roles, seek funding, or advocate for your business, particularly in industries where you are underrepresented. On the flip side, it could propel you to pursue these goals relentlessly.

This experience can impact you along a spectrum of two extremes. On one end, you may underprice your services or hesitate to seek venture capital, fearing that systemic biases will prevent you from being taken seriously. This can also lead to feelings of helplessness (as discussed earlier) and struggles with long-term planning (as mentioned above). On the other extreme, you might pursue leadership roles and advocacy relentlessly, becoming bold and outspoken, driven by a passion to right a wrong. While this approach can accomplish a lot and isn't inherently bad, it can lead to emotional turmoil and burnout, which can harm your mental, emotional, physical, financial, or relational health.

In our world, there are many systemic biases and problems that are beyond your capacity alone to change, but they do have a massive effect on your life. In this book, as you heal your trauma and pain created from these problems, you'll become more effective at changing them. When we try to change a system from fear and stress responses, we tend to be less effective. By actively engaging in the trauma-healing tools in this book, you'll access the curiosity, courage, and creativity necessary to create a better tomorrow, starting today.

Identifying and bringing awareness of how you may have experienced trauma is the first step in releasing the pain your body is holding so that you can access more clarity, confidence, ease, and, ultimately, success. Over the coming chapters you'll learn to relate to the different parts of yourself that are still holding the pain from these events and support them in healing and navigating this new world—one where safety, connection, and success are consistent flavors of your daily experience.

As Debbie finished the exercise, a chill of fear crept up her spine. She felt an unsettling blend of vulnerability and hopelessness, her chest tight as she considered the weight of it all. A nagging doubt lingered: *What if this work isn't enough? What if I'm destined to feel stuck, frustrated, and unable to truly heal?* She looked around the room, watching others with a glimmer of hope, yet couldn't quite shake the feeling that maybe healing was for them, not for her.

Across the room, Emily's experience was strikingly different. A wave of relief washed over her, as if a heavy, unspoken truth had finally surfaced. *So this is why things have felt so hard*, she thought, breathing deeply, her shoulders relaxing for the first time in days. She felt deeply validated, her struggles finally making sense. There was a gentle reassurance in her chest, a sense that she wasn't alone, and that her journey had meaning.

I reminded both Debbie and Emily that the path forward lies in reconnecting to the Self, as we explored in the previous chapter. By grounding themselves in that stable, wise center within, they could start to feel prepared to face the barriers to trauma healing. With each step into this work, they would unlock more somatic intelligence, strength, and clarity. Together, we were about to venture into the next phase, equipping them with tools to face the common barriers to trauma healing with renewed courage and resilience.

Key Takeaways

- Trauma comes in many shapes and forms, and due to the high-pressure environment, uncertainty, and unique challenges of entrepreneurship, it is often triggered, resulting in blocks to the creativity, innovation, and sustainable working methods needed to create impactful, profitable businesses without sacrificing individual or collective well-being.

- Trauma and fear responses can be learned through personal, lived experience and can also be passed down through generations via epigenetic mechanisms, affecting how you navigate success, leadership, and money, especially for females and minorities.

Now that you have identified how your trauma influences your access to success and ease, in the next chapter, you'll create your action plan to move past your personal patterns of protection that create barriers to healing trauma.

Chapter 8

Common Barriers to Processing Trauma

Debbie was busier than ever, burying herself in work to numb the discomfort of confronting how deeply trauma—and the drive to achieve as an escape from inner pain—was affecting her life. She reassured herself that her hardships had made her stronger, but the words felt empty. One evening, as she sat curled up with cramps from her IBS, her phone buzzed with a message from a mutual friend who had recently spoken with Alex. After a hesitant pause, the friend shared that Alex had mentioned feeling like things had drifted so far apart that they were wondering if separation might be best. Debbie's heart sank; she'd sensed the growing distance, but hearing that Alex was also contemplating separation left an ache in her heart and she felt shaken.

Emily, on the other hand, kept her trauma at arm's length, analyzing her feelings from a distance rather than allowing herself to truly experience them. Although she diligently set intentions to build her self-confidence, her tendency to micromanage her assistant eroded the trust she was trying to foster. This compulsion for control extended to her relationship with her fiancé, fueling frequent disagreements over wedding details and deepening her anxiety as she struggled to balance her need for perfection with an unsettling sense of disconnection.

Neither Debbie nor Emily realized that they were encountering common barriers to processing trauma. They hadn't done anything wrong; they simply couldn't yet see that there was a gentler way to achieve their goals and make a meaningful impact without sacrificing their mental or physical health or compromising their values. As Debbie and Emily sat down to their next BBB session, I shared that we'd be covering common barriers to processing trauma.

Sometimes, the body instinctively tries to avoid processing trauma to protect itself from revisiting the pain, yet unprocessed trauma doesn't simply vanish; it becomes stored in the body's tissues and nervous system. Dr. Bessel van der Kolk, a renowned trauma expert, has shown through his research that trauma lodges itself in the body, often manifesting as physical and emotional tension until it's addressed.[13]

Healing, then, isn't about forcing ourselves to revisit every painful experience but about recognizing our unique protective patterns and gently working around them and with them. By identifying, acknowledging, and caring for these patterns, we open the door to a deeper healing process, allowing ourselves to access the lightness and ease that come from living in alignment with our true Self and our somatic intelligence. This will allow you to move from survival to true connection, healing, and leadership in your personal and professional life.

Identifying Protective Patterns

I encouraged Debbie and Emily to identify their protective patterns by reviewing a list of common barriers to trauma healing and noting the ones that resonated. You can do the same. The barriers are organized by core

---

13. Bessel A. Van der Kolk, *The Body Keeps the Score: Brain, Mind, Body in the Healing of Trauma* (Viking, 2014).

themes, making it easier to recognize your own patterns and begin moving past them.

1. Wanting control and structure

Fear of structure

You'll know you're experiencing this barrier if you feel tense or anxious when asked to follow structured routines or healing practices. Structure may remind you of situations where you felt powerless, so even helpful routines may cause muscle tension, shallow breathing, or resistance.

Overstructuring as a defense

You'll know you're experiencing this barrier if you need to know every detail of what's coming next and feel uneasy with uncertainty. You may rely on rigid schedules and systems, and avoid spontaneity, preferring to control every aspect of your healing process.

Procrastination through perfectionism

You'll know you're experiencing this barrier if you spend hours planning, researching, or perfecting tasks rather than actually doing them. You might overthink and delay emotionally difficult tasks, telling yourself that you need to "get it just right" before starting.

Overworking or staying busy

You'll know you're experiencing this barrier if you constantly fill your schedule with work or activities to avoid dealing with your emotions. You may feel a sense of accomplishment, but you're always fatigued, tense, or burned-out from never slowing down.

2. Avoidance and Numbing

Numbing through food, alcohol, or external fixation

You'll know you're experiencing this barrier if you reach for food, alcohol, or other distractions (like helping others solve their problems) to numb or avoid emotional pain. You might feel relief in the moment, but deep down, unresolved feelings are still there, leaving you disconnected from your body.

Minimizing the effects of trauma

You'll know you're experiencing this barrier if you catch yourself saying things like "It wasn't that bad" or "It made me stronger" to avoid addressing the real emotional impact of your trauma. You may downplay how much it still affects you in order to avoid confronting those painful emotions.

Detachment from emotions and physical sensations

You'll know you're experiencing this barrier if you tend to rationalize your emotions or attribute them to something else. Rather than feeling your body's reactions (tight chest, butterflies, tense shoulders), you might blame external factors like stress from work or not enough sleep.

Fear of feeling out of control

You'll know you're experiencing this barrier if you're afraid to let yourself fully experience emotions like sadness, anger, or grief because you worry you might lose control or break down. To avoid this, you may keep things surface level and shy away from situations that feel too emotionally intense.

3. Intellectualizing and Overthinking

Intellectualizing trauma

You'll know you're experiencing this barrier if you spend a lot of time thinking about your trauma or creating narratives around it, but you avoid feeling the emotional and physical responses that come with it. You may try to make sense of everything logically rather than allowing your body to process the emotions.

Burnout from overintellectualizing

You'll know you're experiencing this barrier if you believe that understanding trauma logically is enough to heal, but you still feel emotionally drained, tense, or physically exhausted. This happens because you haven't allowed your body to release the stored stress that comes with trauma.

Procrastination through perfectionism

You'll know you're experiencing this barrier if you constantly stay in learning mode, gathering information but avoiding the actual emotional work. This is a cognitive escape that keeps you from directly facing the pain and discomfort of your trauma.

4. Fear of Vulnerability and Lack of Safety

Avoidance of vulnerability

You'll know you're experiencing this barrier if you avoid being emotionally open, even in therapy or somatic practices, because it feels too risky. If you've been hurt before when you were vulnerable, it may feel safer to stay detached and intellectual rather than fully opening up.

Lack of safe relationships

You'll know you're experiencing this barrier if you don't feel comfortable opening up to people or lack a support system of trusted individuals. This keeps your nervous system on high alert, making it hard to relax into deeper healing practices. You may feel hypervigilant, always on guard, or unable to fully trust others.

Cultural or familial conditioning

You'll know you're experiencing this barrier if you grew up in a culture or family where expressing emotions was seen as weak or shameful. This conditioning might make you feel guilty or uncomfortable about acknowledging your trauma or expressing vulnerability.

Healing for the Elimination of Pain and the Creation of Success

Now, this might not seem like at first, but it's one of the most common ones entrepreneurs who read this type of book fall into. Attempting to heal something so that you can achieve something (whether that be the elimination of pain, forever, or to be able to write better copy on your ads and do better sales calls) is a micro aggression to yourself and blocks the flow of Self energy. It's a little way we create a "fight" state of dysregulation, meaning everything you do from here is an exhaustive, ineffective effort at healing.

You'll know you're experiencing this barrier if you're reading this book thinking about how it'll make you more productive, better at your job, or even eliminate the anxiety, sadness, and discomfort in your life—forever. Much of the personal development industry markets a promise that healing will erase discomfort forever, suggesting that freedom lies in the elimination of our struggles. On one hand this is true, and on the other, it's harmful and ineffective.

Now, you're allowed to be annoyed at me, or yourself. You may have gotten this far into the book because a part of you can see that you need to heal so you can be more effective, efficient, and successful.

The truth is, you don't reach a place of peace, ease, and relief by pushing or pursuing with the goal of eliminating discomfort. Instead, you need to cultivate a deep admiration, benevolence, and love for the way your body and psyche communicate through things that are uncomfortable. You're not engaging in this process so that you can simply produce amazing content or build a business with three hundred employees. You're not extracting anything from yourself. Instead, You're working to understand you with deep care and respect. This means that as you engage in this work, you need to let go of any agenda to "achieve" something from it.

Your job is to understand your body, care for it, and align with your nervous system. This alignment helps you find success that is right for you, your community, your vision, and the unique gifts and energy you bring into the world.

To build on this understanding, you need a practical tool to develop an action plan that will help prevent these tendencies from taking over. The purpose here isn't to control or suppress these parts of yourself but to support and strengthen your ability to channel energy toward healing and creation, freeing yourself from the grip of old, disempowering patterns.

EXERCISE: Overcoming Barriers to Processing Trauma

This exercise is designed to help individuals identify their personal barriers to processing trauma and create a tailored action plan to address these obstacles. The aim is to promote self-awareness, emotional processing, and healing.

Step 1: Identify your barriers. Reflect on the following questions and write down your responses. This will help you pinpoint specific barriers you face.

- **Overworking and busyness**—do you keep yourself immersed in work to avoid confronting your feelings? How does this affect your well-being?
- **Minimizing past trauma**—are there experiences you tend to downplay or rationalize? What narratives do you tell yourself about these experiences?
- **Intellectualizing**—do you often analyze your trauma without feeling it? What thoughts or theories do you create around your experiences?
- **Detachment from emotions**—are you aware of your physical sensations related to trauma? How do you rationalize your feelings instead of experiencing them?
- **Avoidance of vulnerability**—what practices do you avoid that could help you process trauma (e.g., therapy, meditation)? Why do you think you avoid these?
- **High stress or burnout**—how do you manage your stress? Are you experiencing chronic stress symptoms?
- **Difficulty integrating healing practices**—what trauma-informed practices do you know about? Why do you struggle to implement them?

Step 2: Set your goals. Based on the barriers identified, establish specific, measurable, achievable, relevant, and time-bound (SMART) goals. This is an example:

- **Specific**—I will practice mindfulness for ten minutes each day.
- **Measurable**—I will track my mood and physical sensations in a journal.
- **Achievable**—I will start with three therapy sessions over the next month.
- **Relevant**—This goal will help me process my anxiety more effectively.
- **Time-bound**—I will complete this by the end of the month.

Step 3: Create your action plan. For each barrier, create an action step that aligns with your goals. Here's a template you can use:

Barrier	Action Step	Timeline	Resources Needed
Overworking or busyness	Schedule daily breaks and set work limits.	Ongoing	Timer, calendar
Minimizing past trauma	Write a letter to yourself acknowledging your past.	One week	Journal, pen
Intellectualizing	Attend a somatic therapy workshop.	One month	Research local workshops
Detachment from emotions	Practice body scans to connect with physical sensations.	Daily for two weeks	Guided meditation app
Avoidance of vulnerability	Join a support group or therapy.	Ongoing	Online platforms, local resources
High stress or burnout	Integrate stress-relief activities (e.g., yoga).	Start this week	Yoga app, gym membership
Difficulty integrating healing	Explore one new trauma-informed practice.	Two weeks	Books, online resources, a therapist, coach or mentor

Step 4: Review and adjust. At the end of each week or month, review your action plan. Reflect on your progress and make adjustments as needed. Consider what worked, what didn't, and how you can continue to support your healing journey.

Debbie recognized her tendency to overwork as a way to avoid confronting her emotions. While it made her anxious to commit to not working evenings or weekends, she felt comfortable with a smaller step: allowing herself just five minutes each day to feel her emotions if she wanted to work past her usual hours. This approach let her work with her patterns gradually, acknowledging her pain and trauma while accepting that healing wasn't about diving in perfectly. The goal was to make space and address the underlying pain and fear driving her overworking habits.

Emily found it challenging to stop intellectualizing her trauma. The more she understood herself, the more her quick mind latched onto theories, studies, and facts to avoid feeling her actual emotions— even the comfortable ones! She was already connecting with her Self each morning, so she decided to expand that practice by paying extra attention to her body sensations, letting her mind grow comfortable with her focus shifting inward. Each morning, she spent a few more moments noticing the feelings in her body before starting her day. This small addition was strengthening her ability to feel rather than analyze. As a bonus, her fiancé began noticing how much calmer, softer, and more open she was. This made wedding planning a little more enjoyable as Emily's ability to sit with the uncomfortable sensations all the decision-making was creating meant she didn't feel the need to nitpick her fiancé so much.

Key Takeaways

- Your nervous system's job is to keep you in the familiar spaces and patterns (even if it's causing you harm and stopping you from achieving your dreams). It's natural to experience resistance to looking at deeper trauma, even though it will be supportive for you.

- Unresolved trauma doesn't just disappear—it stays stored in the body and affects physical and emotional health.

- To create the business, life, and health you desire, it's important to learn to move past your own protective patterns. The key to overcoming these barriers is not forcing the healing process but learning to recognize and acknowledge individual protective patterns.

Now that you've created an action plan for overcoming barriers to processing trauma, you're ready to learn emotional alchemy and how to access the innate creativity, wisdom, and maturity that fosters effective, innovative, sustainable, and joyful entrepreneurship.

Chapter 9
How To Process Emotions and Become Wiser

Debbie and Emily were both overwhelmed with tension and anxiety, feeling like their minds were a jumbled mess of scribbles. Debbie started snapping at her virtual assistant, while Emily found herself procrastinating on the harder tasks piling up on her to-do list. Both women messaged friends, expressing frustration, fatigue, and the sense that they were falling behind. Emily was barely keeping up with her inbox, and Debbie's anxiety spiked at the end of sales calls, causing her to freeze and miss closing deals.

They couldn't yet recognize that they were experiencing a heightened emotional response to their work; without processing these emotions fully, they remained under the influence of reactive stories and waves of feeling, unable to access grounded, logical thinking. It's understandable and valid, given the roller coaster of emotions that comes with entrepreneurship. This journey can be profoundly rewarding, offering unique benefits to those who learn to navigate its emotional depths. However, it also brings challenges that other types of work don't usually present.

By Tuesday, Debbie had endured back-to-back meetings that left her so frustrated she felt physically unwell. Instead of reaching for her regulation cheat sheet, she texted a friend: "Come over at 6? I've had a massive day, and I need a glass of wine. Bring cheese?" She skipped our session for wine and cheese—not wrong in itself, but without any emotional processing, Debbie didn't find the relief she was hoping for.

Emily, feeling heavy with the week's demands, joined the session and shared openly in our circle. "Lately, I feel like I'm in between the person I used to be and the person I want to become. When I get triggered or things get tough, it's so tempting to fall back on old negative patterns—and often, I do. I think I need to learn to sit with the tension longer and not react right away, even if it's uncomfortable."

Emily was in the right place; emotional processing (and sitting with the tension) was exactly what we'd be covering that day—and in this chapter.

In today's society, we're often conditioned to ignore, avoid, or push away our emotions; when we do address them, it's common to talk them over until we're exhausted (and perhaps exhausting those around us). The acts of talking about, analyzing, and intellectualizing our emotions do have their place in healing, but they're only a small part of the most effective processing and healing approach.

These are some key signs that you may be intellectualizing or avoiding your emotions rather than fully processing them:

- You have persistent feelings. Emotions seem endless, with little relief. For example, you may still be carrying the disappointment from a failed launch long after it's over.
- You're overthinking. You worry about what you "should" do or dwell on others' opinions instead of listening to your own inner guidance.

- You're highly reactive. You find yourself frequently reacting strongly to situations, even small ones.

- You have chronic dysregulation. Your nervous system feels on edge more often than not, struggling to find a balanced, regulated state.

- You struggle with decision-making. You feel unclear or indecisive, making it challenging to feel confident about your choices.

Studies have shown that avoiding or repressing emotions can significantly impact health, increasing risk of burnout, hopelessness, and even aggression, which has been linked to poorer cardiovascular health.[14] Research even suggests that unprocessed emotions can contribute to early mortality, with connections to conditions like cancer and heart disease.

Along with that, there are many studies that demonstrate how effectively processing emotions can improve your capacity to respond to situations and be resilient in the face of stress, cardiovascular health, access to intuition and somatic intelligence and better decision-making, creative thinking and innovation.[15] As your own personal well-being improves, you get better results in your business, and you create a workplace environment that's nice to be around.

---

14. Daichi Shimbo et al., "Translational Research of the Acute Effects of Negative Emotions on the Cardiovascular System," *Journal of the American Heart Association 13, no. 9* (2023), https://doi.org/10.1161/JAHA.123.032698.

15. Leopold Helmut Otto Roth, Celine Bencker, Johanna Lorenz, and Anton-Rupert Laireiter, "Testing the Validity of the Broaden-and-Build Theory of Positive Emotions: A Network Analytic Approach," *Frontiers in Psychology* 15 (2024), https://doi.org/10.3389/fpsyg.2024.1405272.
Frontiers (2007): 217–238, http://www.jstor.org/stable/27768129; Dandan Tong, Hanxiao Kang, Minghui Li, Junyi Yang, Peng Lu, and Xiaochun Xie, "The Impact of Emotional Intelligence on Domain-Specific Creativity: The Mediating Role of Resilience and the Moderating Effects of Gratitude," *Journal of Intelligence 10*, no. 4 (2022): 115, https://doi.org/10.3390/jintelligence10040115; Jennifer S. Lerner, Ye Li, Piercarlo Valdesolo, and Karim S. Kassam, "Emotion and Decision Making," *Annual Review of Psychology 66* (2015): 799–823, https://doi.org/10.1146/annurev-psych-010213-115043.

Now you know the importance of processing emotions, let's look at *how* to do it. Emotions are energy in motion, and when you allow them to process fully in the body—meaning you ride the wave of sensation and energy until it naturally dissipates—you gain access to new thoughts, a deeper sense of wisdom, and the ability to view things from a fresh perspective. This grounded, wise state supports more effective, innovative, and joyful action, allowing you to work in ways that feel sustainable and aligned. Plus, because you've moved that energy through your body rather than letting it get stored in your cells and nervous system, you feel more regulated—and get more access to somatic intelligence!

You're about to learn the practice of emotional alchemy, a skill you'll use to process trauma and connect with your somatic intelligence. Then, we'll look at the types of emotions you may experience, and finally, we'll dive into how to avoid common barriers when processing your emotions.

Just as we built a strong foundation for trauma healing by connecting with the Self, now we are cultivating the skill of emotional alchemy. This practice increases your capacity to be present with intense sensations and emotions in the body. Later, we'll explore how to get curious, heal, and release. For now, it's simply about allowing the emotional energy to reside in your body and observing what unfolds naturally—it's not about seeking healing or resolution just yet (we'll cover that part of the journey in the chapters that follow). Keeping that in mind, this practice is incredibly healing in and of itself.

EXERCISE: Emotional Alchemy

Emotional alchemy is the practice of fully experiencing emotions in your body to uncover their wisdom and receive any messages they may hold. It's about allowing emotions to exist without pushing them away or trying to fix them, letting them unfold naturally until they reach completion.

Imagine your body as a house and emotions as visitors passing through. Sometimes, these visitors bring insights, helping us understand something about our inner experience or needs. Other times, they have no specific message and simply need to be felt, like a visitor who arrives and then moves on.

The minipractice consists of a short exercise, lasting about two minutes, which you repeat as often as desired. I recommend engaging in these minipractices for twenty to twenty-five minutes at a time, a few times a week.

Step 1: Set up for the minipractice. You don't need a timer, but you might want one. You'll need two minutes, and you'll do one round. I use the minipractice a few times a day. Someone said something that hurt you? Do this practice for two minutes (it's often less), before you respond so that you respond in a way you're proud of. Got a no from a prospective client or investor? Do this practice for two minutes, so that you're more regulated during the day and can learn from the experience.

Step 2: Tune in by bringing awareness to your body and noticing what's present inside.

- Ask yourself "What am I aware of?"
- Look for thoughts, sensations, or emotions, aiming to identify an emotion. If no emotion is clear, find a sensation or thought and ask, "If this were connected to an emotion, what might it be?"
- If you can't identify an emotion, focus on a sensation for the next step while you learn to recognize emotions. This process helps you hold and transform energy within the body instead of letting it fuel the mind.
- If you feel numb, recognize that numbness itself is the sensation. Get curious about it: does it feel tingly, heavy, cold, hollow? Does it connect to feelings like hopelessness, fear, or frustration? Familiarize yourself with your current experience of numbness before moving on to the next step.

Step 3: Allow the emotion, thought, or sensation to be present for ninety seconds. You can choose one of two approaches:

- Focus your awareness on the sensation or emotion in your body. Fully feel it, allowing it to remain in your awareness without resistance. If thoughts arise, set them aside for later.
- Express the emotion physically. Ask, "If I could show someone how this emotion feels in my body, what would I do?" This could involve adjusting your breath, face, hands, or even making a sound. Move or make sounds as feels right.

During these ninety seconds, let the sensation be more present than any accompanying thoughts. Notice if your mind wanders, and practice observing thoughts without engaging. Label them (e.g., thoughts about dinner) and let them be. When you notice you've followed a thought trail, gently return to the question "What am I aware of?" and start again.

For the full practice, set a timer to go off every two minutes for a total of twenty minutes. Each interval involves about thirty seconds of noticing what you're aware of, followed by ninety seconds of experiencing it. Repeat this practice ten to twelve times. In the first thirty seconds of each round, be careful not to compare how you're feeling now to how you were feeling at the start of the last round. You can stay with the same emotion if it's still there, but you can also move to a different emotion or sensation if you feel called to it. This is a judgment-free process.

A meditation app like Insight Timer can help with setting up your timer. Practicing for a longer period of time allows you to access deeper layers of stored emotions within your body.

By the end of the emotional alchemy session, you'll often find a sense of spaciousness. If you sit with it long enough, you may feel ease, bliss, joy, pleasure, or a new perspective on life's challenges. The weight of life and leadership may feel lighter.

This practice can also reveal insights and wisdom directly from your body, such as intuitive nudges about actions to take or avoid, or messages about boundaries. These subtle pieces of information emerge as if gently placed into your awareness—**this is your access to somatic intelligence.**

The Types of Emotions

There are three types of emotions:

Emotions that aren't yours—some emotions you experience may feel like they don't belong to you, and that's because they don't. As we interact with others, our emotional bodies can pick up on the emotions of those around us. Mirror neurons in our brain also see other people's emotional experiences and recreate them within us. Essentially, we absorb emotions from external stimuli, and these emotional energies need to move through our bodies. These emotions often don't carry a big message for us; they simply need to be digested and released.

Core emotions—these emotions feel timeless, like they could last forever. They're existential in nature, part of the human experience, and aren't necessarily here to solve a problem—they just need to be felt. Just as joy is universal, so is sadness. Sometimes, we just need to experience them without overanalyzing or trying to fix anything. These emotions—like loneliness—will always exist within us, shared by all, and we simply need to let them move through us.

Messenger emotions—these are the ones I've been referencing when speaking about extracting wisdom. These emotions carry insights and messages that we can use to guide our actions; however, they often only offer *one* perspective. You don't need to make big decisions based solely on one emotion (though you can if it feels right). Not every emotion requires action, and sometimes it simply needs to be witnessed and felt. However, if an emotion consistently shows up after being processed, it's likely asking for action or change. The more you practice, the easier it will be to identify which emotions need space to be processed and which need action. You'll notice a different "flavor" or sensation in your body that signals this.

Emotions carry messages, and as entrepreneurs and visionaries, we often experience a unique blend of feelings tied to the pressures and sacrifices we face. Below, I've listed some of these emotional experiences, ones that I've personally noticed and others I've observed in fellow entrepreneurs. While these are human experiences, your experience as a visionary has a specific flavor and tone that others who do not have your same approach to work and the world will not experience (just like we can't experience theirs!)

Visionaries' grief

- The life you could have had—a sense of loss for the stability, predictability, or inclusion that might have come with a more traditional career path.
- Self-neglect—recognizing the pain caused by self-criticism, burnout, or neglect, leading to deep emotional fatigue.
- Loss of simplicity—mourning the lighter, less complicated life before entrepreneurship added new layers of complexity.
- Strained relationships—grief over relationships, whether friendships, family ties, or romantic connections, that may have suffered due to business focus.
- Who you once were—mourning the version of yourself you left behind as entrepreneurship reshaped you, emotionally, mentally, or physically.

Visionaries' shame, loneliness, and disappointment

- Missed opportunities—regret or embarrassment over ideas, partnerships, or projects left unexplored.
- Disappointment in yourself—frustration or shame when personal expectations, goals, or timelines aren't met.
- Loneliness in leadership—the feeling of isolation or misunderstanding that comes with the weight of making significant decisions on your own.
- Fear of letting people down—a constant worry about disappointing clients, investors, your team, or even yourself.
- Shame from the fear of failure—in an industry with high rates of failure, shame often surfaces when growth isn't as fast as expected, affecting self-identity and confidence.

The emotions below are more common, and you're bound to experience them simply because you're human, independent of your profession.

1. Happiness
   o Peaceful (calm, content, relaxed) Things are going well; I feel secure.
   o Powerful (confident, successful) I'm achieving something important; I feel capable.
   o Accepted (respected, valued) I feel a sense of belonging.
   o Joyful (playful, energetic) Life is enjoyable, and I'm engaged.

2. Sadness
   o Lonely (isolated, abandoned) I feel disconnected; I need support or connection.
   o Vulnerable (overwhelmed, fragile) I need protection or safety.
   o Guilty (ashamed, regretful) I may have violated my values; I need to make amends.
   o Depressed (empty, powerless) I feel inadequate or helpless; I need help or encouragement.

3. Anger
   o Frustrated (annoyed, agitated) Something is blocking my goals; I need to address it.
   o Aggressive (provoked, hostile) I feel threatened; I need to defend myself.
   o Betrayed (resentful, disrespected) Someone has violated my trust; I need fairness.
   o Critical (skeptical, distant) I disagree with what's happening; I need to voice my concerns.

4. Surprise
   o Confused (perplexed, disillusioned) I don't understand what's happening; I need more information.
   o Startled (shocked, disoriented) Something caught me off guard; I need to get grounded.
   o Amazed (awed, astonished) I'm witnessing something incredible; I need to savor it.

5. Fear
   o Scared (helpless, frightened) I perceive danger; I need protection or reassurance.
   o Anxious (worried, nervous) I'm uncertain about the future; I need to prepare or seek support.
   o Insecure (threatened, weak) I feel vulnerable; I need to strengthen my position.

6. Disgust
   o Disapproving (judgmental, skeptical) I'm not aligned with what's happening; I need to voice my objections.
   o Disappointed (let down, dissatisfied) My expectations weren't met; I need to adjust them.
   o Disgust (horrified, repelled) This situation is not okay; I feel unsettled.

Common Mistakes When Processing Emotions

Below, you'll learn how to avoid the key mistakes that entrepreneurs make when it comes to processing our emotions and how to process your emotions so that you can experience all your wisdom, creativity, and innovation.

Mistake 1: Getting stuck in the thoughts

Thoughts are similar to emotions in that they are a way that energy moves through your body and how your body communicates to you, but they're almost a lower quality, less accurate way of seeing life. What's important to know is that thoughts aren't permanent, rarely represent the full picture or total truth of a situation, and will vary based on the state of your nervous system, emotions, hormones, and environment.

Some thoughts are intentional, like if I asked you to imagine your mom saying "purple elephant." You can think that on purpose, but there are also those random, uninvited thoughts that just pop up. Neuroscience helps explain how thoughts come to be; essentially, neurons in your brain communicate with each other using electrical signals, which is why thoughts can feel so automatic.

But here's the deal—thoughts aren't just things that happen in your head. They actually impact your body and are impacted by your body. They've got a nice, symbiotic relationship going on. For example, a fear-based thought can trigger physical symptoms like a racing heart or muscle tension, while a grounded, confident thought can promote a state of relaxation and ease.

Your thoughts and physical state are in constant conversation—your body can influence your thoughts, and your thoughts can change how your body feels. That's why when we talk about nervous system regulation, we're also talking about getting out of the constant loop of automatic thinking, directing your attention to your body and using it to calm the mind, but also being mindful about the thoughts you feed your body.

Mistake 2: Not letting emotions fully move through your body, which prevents you from accessing their valuable insights and wisdom

Imagine your body is like a house, and emotions are guests who come to visit. Some guests, like joy and excitement, feel like your best friends—you open the door wide and practically beg them to stay. You hold onto those positive emotions, hoping they'll never leave. But just as day follows night (thanks to the law of duality), where there is ease, there will inevitably be discomfort. And those emotions we label as difficult—sadness, anger, anxiety . . . We often think they're like a loud, annoying neighbor who comes by at the worst times. We tend to avoid them, shove them aside, or rush them out the door as fast as possible—big mistake.

Here's the thing: all emotions, whether we call them positive or negative, are simply energy, and energy is neutral. As we confirmed above, emotions carry wisdom, but you can only access that wisdom by allowing the emotion to fully move through your body. When we try to avoid these so-called negative emotions by not welcoming them in, we simply cannot access their wisdom. Plus, they don't just disappear. What happens is that they end up acting very similarly to a toddler begging for attention.

If you ignore or avoid a toddler asking for attention (hopefully you're not doing this to the toddlers in your life), or try to intellectualize with it, they're not going to respond well. They're going to cry harder and throw a tantrum. That's what's happening when you're experiencing migraines or IBS or chronic fatigue—your emotions are trying to get your attention by doing literally *anything* they can through the physiological processes in your body. Eventually, as sad as this is, if you don't address the emotion and look at it, it will stop yelling for your attention, and we stop being able to access that wisdom.

However, when we open the door and allow these emotions to come in and take the time that they need, and we give them a sense of being seen, heard, and held, they can eventually move on and go out the back door, leaving behind a note card of wisdom. That's the process of emotional alchemy that you're about to learn.

Mistake 3: Going outside the window of tolerance

To get the most out of processing emotions and trauma, it's essential to work within what is called your "window of tolerance." Your window of tolerance is the range in which you can feel emotions and sensations without becoming overwhelmed. When you're within this window, you're able to stay connected to both the experience (feeling the sensations and emotions in your body) and a wise, calm presence that allows you to process it.

If you move outside of this window into hyperarousal (overwhelmed, anxious) or hypoarousal (numb, shut down), it becomes difficult to integrate what you're feeling because you're no longer fully present. When emotions are effectively processed within this window, it naturally expands, giving you a greater ability to tolerate and process future emotions or stress.

When you're within your window of tolerance, you are present with the emotion and can manage the experience without feeling overwhelmed. This is where optimal emotional processing happens.

Signs that indicate you are *within* your window of tolerance:

- Emotional state—you feel a manageable amount of emotion and can observe it without feeling flooded.
- Bodily sensations—there is a sense of grounding, your breath is steady, and you can feel emotions moving through your body without feeling stuck or overwhelmed.
- Access to Self—you can think clearly, stay curious, and access experiences of compassion that we discussed in chapter 6. You can reflect on the situation or feeling without becoming lost in the story.
- Ability to say present—you're able to stay present with what you're feeling, without needing to distract yourself or "check out."
- Sense of control—while experiencing emotions, you feel like you are in control and not consumed by the emotions. You can process them while staying connected to your sense of Self.

Signs that indicate you are *outside* your window of tolerance:

When in hyperarousal, you have gone above your window of tolerance. This state is associated with a fight-or-flight response. These are some signs you have entered hyperarousal:

- Emotional state—you may feel overwhelmed, anxious, panicked, or flooded by emotion. You could feel restless, on edge, or angry.
- Bodily sensations—you may experience a racing heart, rapid or shallow breathing, muscle tension, heat, sweating, or a sense of being on fire.
- Mental state—your thoughts may race, and you may become hyperfocused on the worst-case scenario or on escaping the situation. You may have difficulty concentrating or feel trapped in story mode.

- Behavioral signs—you might feel an urge to escape, react impulsively, or distract yourself with something else, like picking up your phone or pacing.
- Sense of control—in hyperarousal, emotions feel overwhelming or like they are taking control of you, leaving you feeling like you need to do something immediately to release the tension.
- Focus on the story—you find yourself going into the story about what happened/what you did/what other people did more than you are focused on experiencing the emotion in your body.

When in hypoarousal, you have fallen below your window of tolerance. This state is associated with a freeze or shutdown response. These are some signs you have entered hypoarousal:

- Emotional state—you may experience numbness, flatness, or emotional detachment. You may feel emotionally checked out or disconnected from the situation.
- Bodily sensations—these may be felt as a slower heart rate, heaviness, fatigue, feeling cold or "frozen," a sense of immobility, or difficulty moving or responding.
- Mental state—you may notice foggy thinking, confusion, dissociation, or zoning out. You may feel like everything is far away, as if you're disconnected from the present moment.
- Behavioral signs—you may want to withdraw, isolate, or shut down emotionally or physically. You might feel paralyzed or stuck in a passive state.
- Sense of control—in hypoarousal, you feel powerless or unable to act. Emotions feel distant, and you may feel overwhelmed by the sense of heaviness or hopelessness.
- Focus on the story—you find yourself going into the story about what happened/what you did/what other people did more than you are focused on experiencing the emotion in your body.

What can you do when you are outside your window of tolerance?

- In hyperarousal, focus on grounding techniques such as slow, deep breathing, pressing your feet into the ground, or doing something that helps you feel connected to the present moment, like focusing on your surroundings.
- In hypoarousal, use activating practices to bring more energy into your body, like gentle movement such as stretching or walking or stimulating your senses by listening to music or using a cool washcloth on your face.

By expanding your window of tolerance through nervous system regulation practices and practicing emotional alchemy regularly, you'll allow the emotion to complete its natural cycle, returning you to a state of safety and opening up more access to the wisdom your body holds. This will naturally increase your capacity to process emotions in a healthy, integrated way, allowing you to stay more often within that "just right" zone where the magic happens.

Mistake 4: Thinking you should feel a certain way

Something that happens a lot, especially when we're just getting comfortable with the process of emotional alchemy, is that we think we should be doing something differently, or we believe we're doing the practice wrong. Chances are, you're probably not doing it wrong. However, by entertaining these thoughts—thinking you're doing it wrong or that there's something else you should be doing—what you're actually doing is staying in your head, focusing on your thoughts rather than the sensations in your body. This makes it harder for the emotion to move through you.

It can be helpful to remember that your body is the house where emotions want to reside. If you've rarely, or never, processed emotions in this way before, you're actually tackling two layers of emotions: the ones that have been stored for years, and the ones that arise in your day-to-day life. This might mean that you experience emotions like anger without fully understanding why. Instead of analyzing or trying to figure out the cause—because that's not emotional processing—could you allow the emotion to move through you? Perhaps it will leave you with some wisdom, or perhaps it won't.

There are three different types of emotions we'll explore below, but for now, what you need to know is that when you're focusing on those "shoulds" or those thoughts of doubt, you're not engaging in the practice. It's your nervous system's way of getting you to avoid the discomfort or uncertainty that comes with emotional processing.

I encourage you to let those thoughts be there—they're allowed—but see if you can consistently redirect your attention back to the questions *What sensations do I feel in my body? What emotion is passing through me?* Keep bringing yourself back to those sensations and emotions, and we'll elaborate more on this below.

Debbie decided to give the emotional alchemy practice a try, but found herself stuck in a looping thought: *I should be further along by now.* Rather than looking beneath the thought for the emotion it carried, she accepted it as truth, letting it weigh heavily on her mind and body as a sign of personal failure. This unprocessed feeling lingered, leaving her feeling weighed down and stuck throughout the workweek.

As Debbie's stress intensified, her IBS worsened. Every meal felt like a risk, triggering painful cramps and waves of nausea that left her hunched over, clutching her stomach, willing herself to keep pushing through. It felt as though her body was betraying her, and the discomfort was relentless. At home, Alex finally sat her down, their voice hesitant yet resolute, broaching the conversation she had dreaded: the possibility of separation. The words filled the air, leaving Debbie numb, then embarrassed, and finally, a deep anger surfaced as she realized her life—so meticulously built—was slipping through her fingers.

Emily, on the other hand, embraced the emotional alchemy practice. Some days, she set aside a full twenty-five minutes to let her emotions flow, fully exploring and understanding them. On busier days, she practiced in micromoments, noticing and allowing her emotions to be present even amid her daily tasks. This approach became invaluable as she navigated wedding planning—she was able to tune in to her emotions, gain insights from them, and handle the challenges of coordinating a big event with newfound ease. Solving problems, balancing family opinions, and managing the logistics felt smoother than ever, even bringing her closer to her soon-to-be mother-in-law. At work, her emotional clarity fostered deeper connections with her team and clients, creating a more collaborative environment.

Through this openness came an exciting opportunity: an invitation to speak on a panel about sustainable tech solutions for social enterprises. It was a perfect fit for her mission-driven business, allowing her to share her expertise in sustainable tech practices with an audience hungry for innovative solutions.

Key Takeaways

- Effectively processing emotions leads to wisdom, creativity, and maturity, which contribute to innovative and sustainable entrepreneurship.

- By allowing emotions to flow through the body without getting stuck in the stories they evoke, you can access deeper wisdom, joy, and creativity in your entrepreneurial journey.
- As humans, we often get trapped by overidentifying with our thoughts or resisting emotions, which hinders access to the insights emotions can provide. Emotional alchemy allows for more intentional and easeful responses.

Integrate this into your life and business by doing the emotional alchemy exercise, so that you can let go of the heavy and difficult emotions you've been holding for months, years, and decades. Next, we'll begin supporting the parts of you that have been suffering, which may manifest as fear of failure, an inner critic, or perfectionism.

Chapter 10
Somatic Trauma Healing

Debbie's mind was flooded with worries as three of her client contracts neared completion. She was convinced that any minor mistakes might cause them to abandon her for a competitor, even though, in reality, they simply didn't need further support. Her heart raced with dread, doubting her abilities and fearing she'd be seen as unqualified.

Meanwhile, Emily felt an overwhelming need to overprepare for her upcoming panel, obsessing over every detail to avoid what she imagined would be public humiliation. She couldn't shake the thought that her friends and colleagues, many of whom she admired, would see her as an amateur. This insecurity had even made her question the Body-Based Business methodology she'd been following; despite experiencing positive results, she had skipped her emotional alchemy practices for days, with a whispering doubt in her thoughts: *What if this isn't as effective as you think?*

When Debbie and Emily arrived, I encouraged them to speak freely, letting their thoughts flow. While their stories were unique, each woman's struggles stemmed from deep-rooted feelings of inadequacy and unprocessed wounds. These core wounds drove parts of them to act in protective ways that were limiting their access to somatic intelligence, sustainability, and innovation in their lives and work—a catch-22, as these very qualities were key to achieving the success they were working toward. Yet, their coping mechanisms, like overthinking and comparison, were blocking that path.

As uncomfortable as this moment was, it was also essential. Now that Debbie and Emily have created safety in their bodies (and so have you!), they are ready to dive into somatic trauma healing. We'll start by exploring the concept of parts, followed by an exercise to help unburden these protective parts, and then we'll open up new levels of somatic intelligence and success.

How Parts Are Created

Parts of us develop in response to challenging or traumatic experiences. When we encounter pain, fear, or discomfort, our system creates parts that take on specific roles to protect us from feeling that pain again. These parts work hard to shield us from reliving old wounds, but in doing so, they can also block us from fully accessing our potential, confidence, and creativity.

Parts are born when we experience something overwhelming or painful, often in childhood, but sometimes even as adults. These experiences don't have to be extreme traumas; they can also be situations where we felt unheard, unloved, unsafe, or inadequate.

The list below has common experiences of pain, and the types of parts they might create inside of you, plus how to know if you're operating from these parts. This is not a comprehensive list, just a way to start piquing your curiosity! How these experiences and parts impact you will vary greatly depending on your life and tendencies.

Abandonment

- Hyperindependent protector—this part pushes you to overwork and avoid relying on others to prevent feelings of abandonment or being unsupported. You'll know you're operating from this part if you overextend yourself, resist delegation, or feel like you can't trust anyone to help you.

- Overworking manager—this part believes that constant work will make you irreplaceable, ensuring you'll never be abandoned. You'll know you're operating from this part if you feel driven to always stay busy to prove your worth.

Betrayal

- Distrustful protector—this part makes you micromanage or control others to prevent betrayal. You'll know you're operating from this part if you avoid deep partnerships, struggle to delegate, and are always wary of others' intentions.

- Hypervigilant manager—this part scans for signs of betrayal, overanalyzing others' actions. You'll know you're operating from this part if you're constantly on edge, mistrusting, or feel the need to control situations to protect yourself.

Rejection

- Perfectionist manager—this part pushes you to perform flawlessly to avoid rejection. You'll know you're operating from this part if you seek external validation, fear criticism, and feel the need to overdeliver on everything you do.

- People-pleasing protector—this part seeks approval by always saying yes and avoiding conflict. You'll know you're operating from this part if you find yourself overcommitting, avoiding confrontation, and prioritizing others' needs over your own to avoid rejection.

Injustice

- Overcompensating protector—this part drives you to work harder and longer to right past wrongs. You'll know you're operating from this part if you push yourself relentlessly, trying to prove you're worthy despite past injustices, which often leads to burnout.
- Victim exile—this part holds the pain of feeling wronged. You'll know you're operating from this part if you feel helpless, adopt a "why me?" mentality, or struggle to break free from feelings of injustice.

Humiliation

- Invisible protector—this part urges you to stay hidden to avoid potential humiliation. You'll know you're operating from this part if you avoid taking risks, prefer to stay out of the spotlight, and fear being judged by others.
- Self-doubting exile—this part holds shame and embarrassment. You'll know you're operating from this part if you doubt yourself, avoid bold moves, or feel overly fearful of repeating past humiliations.

Parentification

- Overresponsible manager—this part feels responsible for everyone and everything, fearing chaos if it doesn't maintain control. You'll know you're operating from this part if you take on too much, feel like you're the only one who can manage things, and become easily burned-out.
- Anxious protector—this part fears that, without control, something will go wrong. You'll know you're operating from this part if you feel anxious when things aren't perfectly organized or micromanage to create a sense of stability.

The Father Wound

- Overworking perfectionist—this part pushes you to strive for perfection to earn approval from authority figures. You'll know you're operating from this part if you feel the need to constantly perform, fear both failure and success, and push yourself to the point of exhaustion.

- Self-sabotaging exile—this part believes you're not good enough and will fail no matter what. You'll know you're operating from this part if you procrastinate, avoid taking risks, or sabotage your success to avoid inevitable disappointment.

The Mother Wound

- People-pleasing protector—this part seeks approval to fill a sense of inadequacy. You'll know you're operating from this part if you prioritize others' needs, struggle to set boundaries, and find yourself burned-out trying to please everyone.

- Criticized child exile—this part holds the pain of not feeling good enough in the eyes of a mother figure. You'll know you're operating from this part if you feel deep self-doubt, avoid taking risks, and struggle to assert yourself in your business.

These parts take on protective roles to keep you safe, but over time, they can become extreme and rigid in their efforts. They believe they need to stay in control because they're holding onto old burdens of fear, shame, rejection, or other unresolved emotional pain.

How Parts Get Triggered

In situations where the stakes are high (like Debbie losing clients or Emily preparing for an important speaking engagement), parts are easily triggered because they influence how the nervous system perceives the information, and they see it as a threat. Through the limited perspective of a part, Debbie and Emily weren't simply at risk of losing a client, or making a mistake on stage, they were at risk of reliving gut-wrenching pain (abandonment, rejection, or failure).

- Debbie's **impostor syndrome part** was triggered, telling her she's not good enough and convincing her that her clients would leave and she'd fail, much like how she may have felt rejected or unsupported in her past.
- Emily's **perfectionist part** was activated by the upcoming panel, fearing she'd be judged as incompetent, similar to past experiences where she may have felt humiliated or inadequate.

Here's how Debbie's and Emily's parts were playing out in this new level of business, responsibility, and decision-making.

Their nervous systems were wired to avoid this kind of emotional pain—and so is yours. Therefore, they had shifted into protection mode, reinforcing these limiting beliefs as a way to stay safe from potential rejection or failure.

It's key to remember that we're often not afraid of the task itself; rather, we fear the sensations or emotions we anticipate will come up when we engage with it. In this case, their bodies were reacting to the threat of painful emotions resurfacing, mistakenly seeing these protective thoughts as the safest option.

Their parts' noble goal to protect them ended up perpetuating the same pain they were designed to shield against. By clinging to fear-based beliefs, Debbie and Emily remained stuck in patterns that blocked their healing and growth—avoiding opportunities, self-sabotaging, and staying anxious. This created a self-fulfilling cycle: the very things they feared (like failure or rejection) became more likely because they couldn't step back and challenge their beliefs. Their nervous systems and protective parts were doing their best to keep them safe, but in the process, they limited access to resilience, creativity, and genuine healing.

The only way to break this cycle and move toward greater success was for Debbie and Emily to regulate their nervous systems, release the original pain, and care for these parts with love, providing them with the support they needed to face past traumas. By becoming an anchor for their fearful parts, those parts could relax and loosen their protective grip, allowing Debbie and Emily (and you!) to access clarity, creativity, confidence, and ease.

So, how do we release this pain and truly heal? First, let's be clear—you don't need to eliminate your fears or unhelpful habits and patterns. When you feel the urge to get rid of these behaviors, it's likely a part of you at work, rather than your Self. When we operate from the Self, we naturally begin to heal, care for, and unburden our parts by understanding their role and offering them the love and attention they need. This process allows the Self to lead with calm, creativity, confidence, and all the qualities we explored in chapter 6.

As these protective parts become unburdened, the nervous system experiences a new sense of safety and views the world as a place of opportunity. By consistently unburdening your parts, you'll not only feel more at ease but also become more equipped to make decisions, lead teams, and grow your business in a sustainable and joyful way.

EXERCISE: Mapping Your Parts and Connecting from Self Energy

After completing the emotional alchemy exercise, you may notice there are some sensations, emotions, and thought processes that don't dissipate after sitting with them for a few minutes. This lingering experience is often a part of you trying to communicate or get a need met.

At this point, we can move into parts dialoguing to engage with this part of yourself more deeply. Start by anchoring yourself in Self energy—the calm, compassionate, and curious qualities of your core Self—so you can approach this part without judgment. Then, continue with the steps below to explore and connect with the part that's seeking your attention.

In this exercise, you'll create a parts map which will help you identify the different parts of you that block your business-building journey, so that you can begin healing and find your unique success without compromising your mental or physical health, or your values.

Step 1: Find a quiet space and center yourself.

Begin by grounding yourself in a calm, relaxed space. Take deep breaths, focusing on embodying the qualities of the Self: curiosity, compassion, calmness, and clarity. This step ensures you are approaching your parts from a place of Self.

Step 2: Identify your parts.

As you reflect on the sensation, emotion, or thought that has lingered, ask yourself, *If this experience were coming from a part of me, what might it be?*

Common parts often include the overwhelmed part, the impostor part, or the perfectionist part. For example, the perfectionist may show up in thoughts that push you to overdeliver or constantly strive for more. You can use the list provided earlier in the chapter as a starting point or guide, but listen to your body first. Your part may be something not on the list. Jot down the name or qualities of this part if it helps.

Sometimes, this can be hard and it's often because of one of two reasons. The first reason is that part of you is holding numerous emotions and opinions. For example, say you feel conflicted because you both want to move across the country but also stay in your hometown. At first, it might feel like both of these desires are coming from one confused and indecisive part. But if you look deeper, it's actually two parts, each with their own desire, creating an experience of indecision.

The second reason is that sometimes we see a part of ourselves through another part and not the energy of the Self. This might look like feeling judgmental toward a part of you, frustrated at it, feeling hopeless toward it, or annoyed at it, or even feeling it's particularly good, helpful, and positive. In other cases, a part of you may be avoidant of other parts of you (such as the part of you that wants to avoid looking at the pain from your last breakup). We call these *interfering parts* and in the next step, we'll address how to unblend from them and relate to all your parts from the qualities of your Self and a regulated nervous system, so that you can access the soft, healing, empowering state within that creates a sense of freedom, well-being, and success.

Check in. Before moving on to each step, come back to your feeling of Self while embodying the qualities you've been practicing since chapter 6. We do this to make sure you're addressing your parts from energy that heals, and also to make sure you're not outside of your window of tolerance.

At times, it will be easy to return to Self, and you'll do it in a few seconds. Other times, it'll take a few minutes, and on other days you'll need to give yourself more space and take a break. When that's the case, pause what you're doing and go do something fun or relaxing and then come back. The key here is coming back intentionally (that's how we know you're not just avoiding the work).

Step 3: Address interfering parts.

In step 2, we spoke about interfering parts, and here we're going to identify them with more depth and clarity, so that you can return to your Self energy more.

Interfering parts are parts of us that feel and look like Self energy (we think we're looking at our parts from our Self perspective), but they've taken over our perception of another part. It's almost like we see ourselves through a different lens—as if we've put glasses on. The process of unblending from interfering parts is like taking the glasses off so that we can see with more clarity.

These are some common interfering parts:

- Judgmental part—does a part criticize or evaluate other parts (e.g., *That's silly, stop whining*)?
- Avoider part—do you feel distracted, spaced out, or want to avoid this process?
- Intellectualizer part—are you analyzing and rationalizing instead of feeling the part?
- Impatient part—is there a part that just wants to rush through this exercise and get it over with?

- Inadequate part—is there a part that feels incapable, like it's not good enough to engage in this work?
- Skeptical part—does a part question the legitimacy of this process or fear painful emotions?

Recognize these parts, acknowledge them, and ask if they are willing to step aside for now so that you can proceed.

Check in. Anchor a little deeper into Self energy, focusing on embodying the qualities of the Self: curiosity, compassion, calmness, and clarity.

Step 4: Map out their physical sensations, emotions, thoughts, and actions.

Once you've identified your parts, start mapping how each manifests in your body and mind.

- Physical sensations—where do you feel tension or discomfort when this part is activated? (e.g., tightness in the chest, tension in the shoulders)
- Emotions—what feelings arise when this part is present? (e.g., fear, anger, insecurity)
- Thoughts—what are the stories or messages this part tells you? (e.g., "I'm not good enough." "I'll fail if I don't do this.")
- Actions— how does this part influence your behavior? (e.g., overworking, avoiding tasks, self-sabotage)
- Job—what is this part trying to accomplish? (e.g., overworking parts might try to give us a sense of control, avoiding parts might try to save us from feeling shame or failure, self-sabotage parts might try to keep us in the same income bracket as Mom and Dad so we feel a part of the family)

Check in. Anchor a little deeper into Self energy, focusing on embodying the qualities of the Self: curiosity, compassion, calmness, and clarity.

Step 5: Focus on and dialogue with your parts.

Now, go deeper into dialoguing with your identified parts, ensuring you're speaking from a state of Self energy (that calm, compassionate, and curious state). Use these prompts:

- **Focus on the part**. Bring your attention to the sensation, thought, or emotion that your part is expressing. Where is it located in your body?
- **Flesh it out**. What does this part feel like? How old does it seem? What emotions or thoughts is it holding onto?
- **Feel Self energy**. How do you feel toward this part? If you feel judgmental, impatient, frustrated, or annoyed, come back to step 2 and remove your interfering parts.
- **Befriend the part.** You can ask the part any questions that naturally come from your own sense of curiosity. Here are some ideas to get you started:
  - What does this part want to be called?
  - How old are they?
  - Do they know how old you are?
  - Would they like to share their story with you?
  - Can they show you where they live (in the shadows, a desert, a cave, etc.)?
  - Would they like to go somewhere else?
  - Where would they like to go?
- **Validate its emotions.** You can do this by reinforcing that, based on their experience and perception, the emotion they're having is valid, natural, and worthy of acceptance. This might look like saying something similar to this:

o "It's completely understandable to feel this way given what you're experiencing."

o "Your feelings make so much sense, and it's okay to feel exactly as you do right now."

o "Anyone in your position would feel the same; this is a natural response."

o "I can see how much this means to you, and it's valid to feel this strongly."

o "It's okay to sit with these feelings—there's no right or wrong way to feel."

- **Explore its job fears**. You can ask the part any questions that naturally come from your own sense of curiosity. Here are some ideas to get you started:

  o How do they protect you?

  o What is their job?

  o How long have they been doing that job?

  o Where did they learn they needed to do that?

  o Who taught them that they needed to do that?

  o What are they afraid will happen if they don't do this job?

  o How would they feel if they didn't have to work so hard?

  o What would they need to be able to stop working so hard?

  o What job would they rather do instead?

  o Are they carrying any pain or hurt?

  o What does their pain look like? Where do they carry that pain in their body?

  o Are they ready to get rid of that pain?

  o In the future, how would they like to get your attention if they need you?

  o Are there any other parts that they work with to protect you?

  o Are there any other parts they dislike?

Check in. Anchor a little deeper into Self energy, focusing on embodying the qualities of the Self: curiosity, compassion, calmness, and clarity.

Step 6: Lead with Self energy.

After dialoguing with your parts, reassure them that you (as the Self) are here to lead. Thank them for their efforts and invite them to trust you to make balanced decisions.

Here are a couple of examples:

- Say to the judgmental part "Thank you for trying to protect me from being hurt or disappointed. But I'm capable of handling this, so it's okay to step back."
- Say to the impostor part "I understand you're trying to shield me from failure, but I can handle both success and challenges."

Step 7: Provide Them Support

The next step is to explore what each part needs and then commit to providing that support in a way that feels genuine and sustainable.

Only make commitments to your parts that you're willing to keep. By doing so, you create a foundation of trust, safety, and confidence within yourself. This internal integrity not only nurtures the relationship with this part but also strengthens your access to your somatic intelligence so that you can achieve sustainable success that aligns with your values and dreams.

- Ask questions such as "What do you need from me?" or "What would make you feel loved and supported?"
- How can you earn their trust?
- How would they like to be loved and looked after?

The answers might be surprisingly simple or more complex. For example, a part might ask for something as small as eating a comforting food that day, like a peanut butter sandwich, to help it feel grounded. Other times, it may need a larger shift, like setting a boundary with someone, saying goodbye to a client, or ending a certain type of relationship. When the request is manageable, go ahead and honor it. If the request feels challenging, see if you can commit to a smaller, related step. For instance, if it's urging you to apply for a new job but that feels like you're abandoning your business, perhaps you can focus on creating more recurring revenue in your current business or reaching out to potential clients to increase your income.

Similarly, if one part encourages you to write a book but your impostor part resists, you don't have to dive into writing immediately. Instead, consider dialoguing with the impostor part to better understand its concerns, building a bridge that might eventually support the writing desire of the other part. (Ask me how I know.)

If you aren't hearing anything from a part when you ask about its needs, it's likely due to a lack of established trust. This is completely natural. Just as you wouldn't expect a child to trust a stranger immediately, it takes time for your parts to open up, especially if they haven't felt safe or heard in the past. By regularly showing up, checking in, and practicing from Self energy through regulation, emotional alchemy, and exercises like these, you gradually build trust. Over time, your parts will feel more comfortable engaging with you, which enhances your access to somatic intelligence and deepens the inner guidance you can rely on.

Debbie sat with her controlling part, a force fueled by anxiety and an unfulfilled need to feel secure and respected. She noticed how it pushed her relentlessly, urging her to manage every detail, oversee every project, and anticipate every possible issue to prevent mistakes. This part demanded that she maintain control at all times, convinced that if she could just manage everything perfectly, she would avoid failure and the sting of disappointment.

Yet, underneath this need for control was a deeper longing—to feel appreciated, capable, and worthy. The controlling part of Debbie's psyche was not only about keeping things in order, it was also a protective layer, shielding her from the fear of being seen as incompetent or inadequate. With each setback, her inner critic would step in, whispering, "You're still not good enough." This only strengthened her resolve to tighten her grip on everything, leaving her exhausted and stuck in a cycle of relentless striving. And so, with every slip or missed expectation, Debbie spiraled deeper into perfectionism, convinced that if she just tried harder and controlled more, she could finally feel worthy and secure.

Her body began to break under the weight. Her IBS pain left her unable to focus and though she tried to push through, the symptoms became too severe, and she found herself being rushed to the hospital. As she lay in a sterile hospital bed, her mind racing, she received a call about her child—there had been more issues at school, ones she'd overlooked, and her child had been suspended. She felt a deep ache realizing that her drive to keep everything perfect in her business had distanced her from her child. Forced to pause her work, Debbie was left to confront the toll her endless striving had taken on her health, her family, and the life she'd worked so hard to build.

The next day, Emily stood in a small garden, dressed in white, surrounded by friends and family, feeling happier than she ever had. Everything had come together beautifully. She was relaxed, filled with excitement as she committed to a life with her best friend, and looking forward to their weeklong honeymoon. Confident that she could fully unwind, without a single thought of work or the future, she felt a deep sense of presence as she noticed the sun filtering through the trees. A swell of joy rose in her chest, and tears of happiness sparkled in her eyes. Having spent the week dialoguing with the part of her that felt skeptical and cautious about embracing this level of success, love, and purpose, she'd found reassurance in reviewing some of the studies presented in the BBB course.

During her honeymoon, Emily noticed she wasn't constantly reaching for her phone or mentally running through her to-do list. She could sit, watch the waves, and feel the sun without the usual nagging feeling of needing to be somewhere else or accomplish something.

On her first day back at work, Emily faced a tough decision regarding a client proposal, a scenario that previously would have caused her days of agonizing. This time, she simply weighed the options, trusted her gut, and made the call, a process that took about four minutes (whereas before it would have taken four days).

In her next team meeting, Emily noticed that her usual inner critic was quieter, allowing her to give direction confidently. Whereas she once worried about how others might perceive her or if she was capable enough, she now felt a steady, grounded belief in her own abilities so she could focus more on achieving the goals than being the person she thought they wanted her to be.

Key Takeaways

- Somatic healing enhances creativity and resilience by freeing up energy to find the creativity, resilience, and ease needed for building a successful and purpose-driven business.

- You can alleviate these struggles by working on nervous system regulation and unburdening past traumas, leading to improved business outcomes, personal well-being, and physical health improvements.

Now that you've mapped your parts out and connected to them from Self energy, you're ready to reshape the way your perception of the world as more empowering and capable of bringing you more abundance and success.

Chapter 11

Beliefs and Success

A few weeks later, on the way to their next BBB session, Debbie and Emily both received an email inviting them to speak publicly about their experiences in the program at an event later in the year. When they arrived at session, they were in drastically different emotional states. When Debbie arrived, she had dark circles under her eyes and her skin looked pale and drained of its usual color. Her posture was slouched, and she moved sluggishly, as if the weight of exhaustion and all her responsibilities were pulling her down. She was still getting to know the pain her long-term dysregulation had caused, and it still felt like her world was slipping out of control. The idea of standing up to share her journey felt like an impossible task—too much with everything she was currently facing.

In contrast, Emily walked in with a bright energy, her posture confident and her face glowing with the kind of calm that comes from rest and excitement. As we got prepped, I noticed she occasionally rubbed her temples and winced slightly, a subtle sign that her migraine had resurfaced despite her upbeat demeanor. I later learned that she'd had this tension since being invited to speak about BBB, and now I can share why.

In that moment, what neither of them realized was that their beliefs about themselves and the world were deeply influencing their responses. These beliefs created the lens through which they perceived safety or threat, essentially determining what their nervous systems deemed worthy of a stress response. By expanding their beliefs, they could broaden their capacity for purpose and success, allowing each of them to approach their business with a deeper sense of alignment and resilience.

The Truth About Beliefs

Beliefs can sometimes appear similar to nervous system stories, but they're a little deeper than that. They are the underlying reason our nervous system creates those stories. Our beliefs allow us to experience fewer unhelpful fear-based stories and more helpful ones from a place of safety. When we have supportive beliefs, we spend less energy on regulation, experience more connections and opportunities, and essentially get more of what we want in the world while feeling better as we do it.

Beliefs are not truths. In fact, nothing is 100 percent true all of the time, even this statement. We choose what to believe based on what is empowering to us in that phase of our life and environment.

Beliefs are patterns or perceptions that shape how we interpret and respond to the world, deeply tied to the state of our autonomic nervous system. These beliefs are not just abstract ideas; they are embodied, meaning they affect and are reinforced by our physical, emotional, and physiological states. Beliefs will influence they way we move our physical bodies and even how we breath. For instance, someone who believes they're not safe might habitually hold tension in their shoulders (their muscles are consistently contracted and bracing in preparation to attack a threat) or have a contracted chest (their body is pulling a vulnerable organ—the heart—away from the world). Someone who believes that it's not safe to stand out might pull their shoulders forward and curve their spine to appear smaller and not be seen by a threat.

Beliefs can develop as survival mechanisms in response to trauma or challenging experiences. For instance, a belief that money is scarce may form as a nervous system adaptation to past financial instability. This belief can be supportive by encouraging careful spending when resources are tight; however, it can become disempowering if it prevents you from taking opportunities that could lead to growth, or if it causes daily anxiety about money, regardless of what's in your account. Similarly, if we grew up feeling unsafe, our nervous system might adopt beliefs like "the world is dangerous" or "I can't trust people," priming us to stay on high alert and prepared for a fight, flight, or freeze response.

As experiences repeat over time, our nervous system creates shortcuts, forming conditioned responses. For example, if failure or rejection repeatedly triggers stress, the nervous system may establish beliefs like "I am not good enough" or "I'll never succeed." These beliefs once served to shield us from situations we didn't have the tools to handle (for instance, avoiding rejection when we didn't realize that a no often reflects the other person's needs rather than our own worth). But as our circumstances change, these once protective beliefs may become limiting, particularly in contexts like entrepreneurship where growth requires embracing uncertainty.

If we develop the belief that we're not good enough as protection from failure, what we're actually protecting ourselves from isn't the event itself, but the anticipated sensations associated with it, like sadness or disappointment. The nervous system steers us away from these experiences, not because they're truly dangerous, but because it doesn't yet recognize that we can feel these emotions without becoming dysregulated. This is exactly why I've prepared you to shift your beliefs by increasing your ability to find wisdom and ease in challenging emotions through emotional alchemy.

Let's consider a belief that can be both empowering and disempowering depending on the context: I can learn from any challenge. This belief can foster resilience, encourage curiosity, and help keep you solution-oriented, even when adversity arises. However, in contexts where self-care and boundaries are essential, this same belief might lead you to overextend yourself or stay in unhealthy situations, driven by the assumption that every challenge must be tackled head-on instead of recognizing when it's time to step back or say no.

The Reticular Activating System (RAS)

To be clear, this isn't new-age pseudoscience; there's a neurological basis for it. Beliefs are linked to the reticular activating system (RAS), the part of the brain that helps manage our fight-or-flight response and filters for perceived opportunities and threats. It sifts through the constant stream of information we receive, focusing on what we direct our attention to—all automatically and without conscious awareness.

In summary, and for the purposes of this book, the RAS has three goals:

- Activate or regulate fight or flight.
- Prove your expectations right by filtering the world through the beliefs you have about the world.
- Find evidence that reinforces your beliefs. For example, if you think you're a bad communicator, you probably will be. If you think you're extremely efficient at your work, you probably will be.

Activating Fight or Flight

The RAS plays a critical role in governing the fight-or-flight response by regulating arousal and modulating the autonomic nervous system and somatic responses. The RAS filters sensory information and helps coordinate responses to stressors, working with the limbic system and hypothalamus to trigger changes like increased heart rate and heightened alertness. During a fight-or-flight response, it integrates emotional states and physical actions, ensuring the body reacts appropriately to perceived threats by altering postural control and other motor functions.

The RAS either creates a stress response or does not and then influences our ability to respond to stress and our body's stress response.[16]

Prove Your Expectations Right

When you set your sights on a goal or an experience you deeply desire, or even just something you're curious about, your brain will work behind the scenes to help you achieve it. Debbie decided to test this out. As the days went on, she chose to focus on the question "How am I going to feel more confident today?" and her RAS started searching for an answer—even though it was not immediately obvious. It's like planting a seed that will grow over time, and you might notice the answer twenty-four, forty-eight, or even seventy-two hours later in subtle ways.

Emily didn't pay particular attention to this homework, but her RAS was still working. When she woke up, she felt the same "something will go wrong" energy from earlier. She told herself that the day was going to be terrible. From there, she began noticing all the ways the day was

---

16. Karlee J. Hall, Karen Van Ooteghem, and William E. McIlroy, "Emotional state as a modulator of autonomic and somatic nervous system activity in postural control: a review," *Frontiers of Neurology* 14 (2023), https://doi.org/10.3389/fneur.2023.1188799; "RAS (Reticular Activating System)," Trauma Research UK, traumaresearchuk.org, accessed December 19, 2024, https://traumaresearchuk.org/ras-reticular-activating-system.

going wrong. She spilled her coffee, missed a meeting, and sat in three traffic jams. And by the end of the day, she was deflated and convinced everything was working against her. Why? Because our brains are wired to prove our expectations right.

Studies show that when we believe we're competent, or lucky, or capable, we experience more positive outcomes such as enhanced performance in maths and reading,[17] we achieve more of our goals, and have increased well-being and improved relationships.[18] Why? Because your brains are constantly scanning for ways to prove your deepest beliefs right; what you expect becomes your reality. Your brain, through your RAS, filters out information it doesn't need and focuses on what you're looking for. So, if you actively decide to focus on confidence, luck, or success, your brain will work to bring more of those things into your life. By consciously choosing where to direct your focus, you have the power to change what feels real to you.

Find Evidence for Your Beliefs

We know the nervous system's main concern is keeping you alive with minimal energy expenditure. It's consistently asking "Am I safe, am I loved?" because being safe and loved keeps you (1) alive and (2) a part of the tribe that will care for you and keep you alive. We also know that your beliefs are the structures your psyche uses to make sense of life and navigate the uncertainty. They're almost like the tool your body uses to fix the problems and concerns of life. Therefore, the RAS and the nervous

---

17. Corinna Peifer, Pia Schönfeld, Gina Wolters, Fabienne Aust, and Jürgen Margraf, "Well Done! Effects of Positive Feedback on Perceived Self-Efficacy, Flow and Performance in a Mental Arithmetic Task," *Frontiers in Psychology 11* (2020), https://doi.org/10.3389/fpsyg.2020.01008.

18. Sarah Schneider, Thomas Lösch, Daniel Schneider, and Astrid Schütz, "How Self-Concept, Competence, and Their Fit or Misfit Predict Educational Achievement, Well-Being, and Social Relationships in the School Context," *Collabra: Psychology 8,* no. 1 (2022): 37154, https://doi.org/10.1525/collabra.37154.

system will be more inclined to seek out or filter information that aligns with those beliefs even if they're disempowering, reinforcing the sense of predictability, control, and (you guessed it) safety.

Plus, by finding evidence to support the current beliefs, your RAS works with your entire nervous system to create a world where it can conserve energy and doesn't need to waste resources processing conflicting information. It filters out what's not relevant to your existing beliefs and focuses on what's familiar, creating an efficiency in cognitive processing. The RAS acts like a gatekeeper, allowing in only the information that aligns with what your brain deems important or true. When you expand your beliefs, you can teach your RAS to focus on what you want to reinforce in your life.

EXERCISE: Expanding Your Beliefs

Start by describing a situation you're struggling with, like public speaking, and then add the word *because* at the end. Finish the sentence out loud.

Example:

I can't do public speaking because _____.

Complete this several times for the same topic. Don't judge your answers—just let them flow. This helps you identify your limiting beliefs. Write down whatever comes to mind.

Examples:

I can't do public speaking because I'm bad at communicating.

I can't do public speaking because it gives me anxiety.

I can't do public speaking because I need to heal my anxiety first.

I can't do public speaking because then I'll be even more disconnected from my friends, and I'll have to work really hard, miss out on things, and they won't understand me. (These statements don't need to be logical!)

From this, you can identify the limiting belief: you're bad at communicating or you need to heal your anxiety first.

Emily, for example, believed that her best friends would judge her when she spoke. Her body interpreted this belief by going into fight mode to protect herself, and she felt tension in her throat. She also believed that the tension meant she wasn't capable, reinforcing thoughts that led to a fight-or-flight response, creating more physical stress.

To interrupt this cycle, first, you can stop the stress response by using the Nervous System Cheat Sheet PDF. Then use the emotional alchemy practice to process the emotion in your body, and then, move to the practice below: expanding your beliefs.

Expanding Your Beliefs

Choose a belief from above. Let's use "I can't do public speaking because then I'll be even more disconnected from my friends, I'll have to work really hard, miss out on things, and they won't understand me." Ask yourself, who or what you would be without this belief? Drop all of your judgments and expectations. Notice what is revealed.

From this space, use curiosity to explore alternative truths. Can you find a new, empowering belief? It doesn't have to be the complete opposite, but can you find something that is as true or truer than the original thought?

- I can still maintain my friendships while pursuing my public speaking goals.
- My friends will support me and understand my commitment to growth.
- I don't have to lose balance between work and connection. I can find harmony.
- I can communicate with my friends about my journey, and they may even feel inspired.

The new empowering belief is this: "My friends will support my growth, and I can find ways to balance both public speaking and maintaining our connections."

Find at least three real, specific examples of how this new, empowering belief is already true for you. This will help you shift your perspective and find peace in this new belief.

1. When I told my best friend about wanting to do public speaking, she was excited for me and even offered to come to my first event to cheer me on.
2. I've taken on new challenges before (like starting my business), and my friends were always understanding and proud of my efforts, even when I had less time to spend with them.
3. I've seen people in my circle successfully balance work, growth, and friendships—there's no reason I can't do the same.

Take a moment to visualize adopting this new belief. Imagine this version of you who truly believes that your friends will support you and believes that you can balance growth with connection. How does this version of you walk? How does this version speak? How do you feel in your body, especially when approaching a public speaking event?

Feel that sense of ease in your body. Let it sink in. How does this new belief shift how you breathe? How would you stand if this belief was 100 percent true? What is one action you can take, in this moment, from the understanding that your new belief is true and real?

It's important to take action on your beliefs because this is part of how we create the information the body needs to see that they are true. Basically, even if I tell myself my friends will still love me if I share my mind on social media but I never do it, my body will never have enough evidence to support the new belief and it'll feel like you're always convincing yourself of something.

However, if I take action from that place (even if I am nervous and scared) the body will then see and experience that it is in fact safe, and the RAS will pick that piece of information up, store it for later, and . . . voilà, you have now embodied the new belief!

Sometimes, you might slip back into old beliefs. Embodying and expanding beliefs is a practice and an experiment—not a goal to achieve. You will, at some point, find yourself falling into believing outdated and disempowering beliefs. Good news: your nervous system is functioning well and pulling you into the familiar—yay! When this happens, here are three steps you can follow that will pull you back into empowering beliefs with as little friction, discomfort, and energy as possible.

1. Celebrate that you saw yourself doing this! The fact that you caught yourself is a massive celebration in and of itself because, not only does it mean your nervous system is doing its job, it

means that you're far enough away from the old belief that you have enough space to see yourself in it. We can't see the things we're in because we're too close to them, so the fact that you caught this means you've made progress in disentangling from your disempowering belief. Do a dance, buy yourself a cupcake, or message your best friend a funny GIF to celebrate that you've see this. Great work!

2. Falling back into old beliefs or patterns of behavior often comes with some sticky emotions or thoughts. These might be disappointment, frustration, disgust, self-judgment, sadness, or frustration. This is natural and to be expected. Feel these emotions in your body, and allow them to move through you by practicing emotional alchemy.

3. Embody, again. Return to the last step of the expanding beliefs practice with the empowering belief you're practicing and embody it. You've got this. Over time, the more you do this, the more familiar your body becomes with this belief and new way of experiencing life, and the more automatically it will reach for the new, empowering belief. It'll get so easy, it'll become automatic.

There are certain empowering beliefs that are necessary for successful entrepreneurship. After coaching hundreds of entrepreneurs, I've seen that the ones who have the most success either already hold, or work on integrating and embodying, key beliefs such as the following:

1. It's possible to achieve success without compromising health, values, or authenticity.

2. Success is not a one-size-fits-all blueprint but defined by each business and individual.

3. Our biology (in which the nervous system is a key player) shapes the way we think, live, interact, work, and perceive the world.

4. There is an intelligence inside of each individual in the world that follows the laws of nature: that everything can live in abundance and harmony together.

5. Following our somatic intelligence creates a pathway for us to find our unique place in the world, the place where we feel alive with the energy of life—purpose, abundance, peace, and joy. It also teaches us how to engage with the 3D parts of the world, such as our work, money, and vision.

Now, these are just insights my brain has picked up, likely based on my own beliefs, which were formed through childhood and personal experience. Think of them as trying on a jacket—see how they fit, how they move, how they flow. Go out and experiment. See what you learn, what feels right, what feels supportive, and what creates more ease, prosperity, and power in your life. If they work for you, keep them. You can also tailor them to suit your life and body, or you can discard them.

The goal is to give you a starting point, using my experiences and the studies I've done with clients, so you can create your version of success, build a business aligned with your values, and bring good into the world. This is exactly what I recommended to Debbie and Emily and, of course, they each took their own unique approaches.

Debbie sat that evening with a glass of wine in hand and a house that felt cold with its emptiness as she faced the reality of her life falling apart. Her phone had emails from the school in the notifications bar, and she couldn't bring herself to read them and be confronted again with her child's suspension. She felt like she'd failed at parenting. The idea of adding a public speaking gig to her to-do list was too much so she politely declined the invitation, furthering her feelings of failure, self-doubt, and regret. She resolved to focus on the basic things—getting clients, dealing with her health, and going to therapy.

Emily sat cozied up on her couch preparing for her speaking event by using her emotional alchemy practice to alchemize the fear her imposter syndrome was experiencing, and the expanding your beliefs practice to embody new beliefs that made her feel confident and prepared. The closer the event came, the more she noticed how her beliefs had shifted—she no longer feared judgment the way she once had. Instead, she saw this as an opportunity to share her vision and passion for sustainable tech solutions. This new, empowering belief helped her stay focused, creative, and confident during the engagement, which led to an impactful presentation. She delivered her message with ease, surprising even herself with how comfortable she felt in front of an audience.

Key Takeaways

- Beliefs aren't just mental constructs; they are deeply tied to the autonomic nervous system and influence how we respond to the world based on past experiences, including survival mechanisms and trauma.
- Beliefs can either empower us by opening doors to opportunities and growth or disempower us by limiting our capacity to act in our best interests or take advantage of opportunities due to fear or doubt.
- The RAS filters information based on what we believe and expect. This means our beliefs can unconsciously direct our focus and influence what we notice or ignore, reinforcing either positive or negative outcomes.

Now that you've identified, and begun to change, your disempowering beliefs, you are ready for a very delicious part of the practice—expanding your nervous system capacity for success and ease.

Chapter 12

Expanding Your Nervous System Capacity for Success

Debbie had made some progress by getting back to basics—securing clients, improving her health, and attending therapy—which had helped her get back on her feet. While she was keeping things afloat, she felt numb, anxious, and negative about life. Most of her free time was spent complaining and planning.

Meanwhile, Emily was cruising along but noticed that the habits she'd adopted to regulate her nervous system were beginning to feel like a chore, causing boredom, frustration, and dwindling motivation. She'd signed a larger contract at a higher price and given herself a generous bonus as a result, and now her free time was spent online shopping, buying things she didn't need. When they arrived at her doorstep, she barely used them—she clearly didn't want them that much either.

What neither woman could see was that this was a nervous system response to sudden change, triggering an impulse to return to normal. For Emily, this meant spending money as fast as she made it, and for Debbie, it meant stagnating in her work as much as she could—ways of bringing themselves back to their original comfort zone. Learning to expand their nervous system capacity by managing self-sabotage would be key to maintaining progress.

Debbie's negativity made it hard to finish her work, so when she arrived at the next BBB session, she felt overwhelmed, hadn't finished last week's to-do list, and sensed her stress creeping back to the level it was in her corporate job days. She was dying to just do nothing, and social media told her to listen to her body and relax—which meant things didn't get done at work, and the growth of her business was already beginning to stagnate.

Emily was struggling to find the energy, excitement, and passion she'd had when she started, but just wanted to go shopping. Because of this disconnection, she ended up postponing her big meetings, investing less in her personal development, and indulging more in buying clothes and food, which she ended up feeling guilty about. She also struggled feeling motivated to come to our session, thinking, *What's the point?*

As Debbie and Emily sat down for class, the projector displayed a question that caught their attention: Why do smart and healthy people self-sabotage? They both felt a twinge of curiosity, thinking *Have I been self-sabotaging too?*

I had planned this class for this exact moment because, after years of supporting people with nervous system dysregulation, I've watched hundreds of entrepreneurs, founders, and professionals transform. They go from feeling on edge, rushed, exhausted, and burned-out to calm, confident leaders, able to bring in income and create change without constantly worrying about money.

In their journey to become resilient and excited to wake up on a Monday morning, there's one common challenge they all face: the nervous system's upper limit.

I've encountered it myself many times—especially while writing this book. I had to catch myself falling into self-sabotage, root down into my body, and reconnect with the leader and author I am.

I couldn't have done it without understanding what I'm about to share with you in this chapter. It's what's happening for Emily and Debbie, and what may be happening for you.

The nervous system's upper limit refers to the amount of pleasure, safety, abundance, and joy that your body feels it is safe to receive. The nervous system is wired to prioritize the familiar because that's what it perceives as safe. When you experience more pleasure or abundance (such as money or recognition) than you're used to, your body might reject it by avoiding or sabotaging it or reducing other areas of your life to maintain balance. This happens because your nervous system recognizes the law of duality: for every experience of bliss or abundance, there is the potential for the opposite—pain or scarcity.

For example, perhaps in the past, you had a great job that was unexpectedly taken away due to circumstances beyond your control, leaving your nervous system unsettled. Or, more deeply rooted, maybe as a baby, you experienced a moment of connection with your mom, only for her to suddenly pull away. These experiences create a nervous system upper limit that dictates how much goodness it allows you to receive, and when you hit that limit, it gives you thoughts, emotions, and impulses that prevent you from going beyond it.

Sometimes this upper limit feels like abundance or joy, but often it feels like sameness or boredom. You might find yourself engaging in behaviors that diminish what you've worked hard to achieve. For some, this looks like procrastination, perfectionism, spending sprees, or even physical ailments like migraines or autoimmune issues. It's as if your nervous system pushes you back into the comfort zone of scarcity or dissatisfaction because it doesn't feel safe to experience prolonged abundance.

For instance, when Emily made a lot of money, she found herself spending it impulsively on things she didn't need, almost as if trying to return to her original financial state. She remarked, "This is basically a trauma response to safety and well-being." And it is—your nervous system perceives the abundance as unsafe, triggering a stress response that leads to behaviors causing actual financial stress, bringing you back to square one.

Many people try to address this through mindset work or therapy, which can help, but the root issue is a pattern embedded in your nervous system. The key is teaching your body that it's safe to receive and keep this abundance. By consistently affirming that this new level of safety and connection is okay, your nervous system can adapt and allow you to experience more ease and flow in your life. Your business can reach its goals more effortlessly, and you'll have more energy to invest in the things that truly matter to you.

The following expansion practice will teach you how to rewire your nervous system to feel safe at this new level of abundance, so you can break free from the cycle of self-sabotage and step into a life of ease, flow, and success.

EXERCISE: The Expansion Practice

For this practice, we are assuming that you are already regulating your nervous system (pillar 1) and addressing and processing your deeper fears and core wounds that we named in the prior chapters, so that you can release a lot of the pain, fear, and discomfort you experience. This expansion practice will be your go-to practice to increase the amount of yummy goodness—pleasures, successes, and joy—in your life.

Now, I'm using the word *expansion* here metaphorically, not literally. We are not literally expanding the nervous system in your body. Instead we are "holding the pose." As we know, your body is a house for experiences, emotions, thoughts, and sensations. To hold the pose means to maintain yourself in a posture for an extended amount of time, despite experiencing discomfort, until the posture feels more natural and easy. In this phase of your journey, you'll learn how to hold the pose of success, joy, abundance, and accomplishment until your body surrenders into the fact that it is safe, and that while, yes, it can experience fear and skepticism, that doesn't mean it needs to avoid success by sabotaging it.

Holding the pose means to root into your Self—the wise one who can experience all of life with resilience and regulation and love. It involves a physical, mental, emotional, and even spiritual grounding.

Preparation for The Expansion Practice:

Identifying your "Why"

Since you've done so much work on regulating your nervous system, healing your trauma, and understanding the different parts of yourself, it's time to ground into a new why.

Your why is the deep, personal reason that fuels your drive to pursue your goals. It's not just a motivator—it's the core of your purpose, what gives meaning to everything you do. Your why connects your actions to your values and desires, guiding you toward the vision you have for your life and business. It brings clarity and alignment to your efforts, making even the hardest challenges feel worthwhile because they are in service of something that truly matters to you.

Your why also creates ease and certainty. It's the thing that makes you feel *I've got this, I know what I'm doing, and I know where I'm going!* It generates a sense of flow; your purpose feels clear and aligned with your actions. It feels like that deep exhale of relaxation, or a fire in your belly that keeps you moving forward. While everyone's why looks different, it tends to bring a similar sense of ease and focus, like a calm confidence that you're on the right path. Some people may call this their purpose.

Up until now, you may have pursued your work due to unhealthy mechanisms and trauma responses, such as trying to heal others in an attempt to also heal those parts of yourself, or to prove to your father that you're smart. Since you've learned to care for those parts and process their emotions, those painful parts won't be pushing you so hard any more. Unless you integrate a new why, you'll struggle to find the motivation and energy to do your work.

Use the following questions to create a new sense of purpose and direction—your why:

What problem or need do I feel passionate about solving through my business, and why does it matter to me personally? This prompt helps you identify the personal connection and sense of purpose behind the work you're doing. Reflect on what experiences, values, or injustices in your life motivate you to create change through your business.

How do I want my business to impact the lives of my clients or customers, and what change do I hope to see as a result of my work? This question encourages you to consider the broader long-term impact of your work on others. Your why is often deeply tied to the value you bring to those you serve.

When I picture myself five years from now, what do I want my life and business to look like? How will it align with my core values and long-term vision? By visualizing your future, this prompt helps you clarify how your business goals align with your personal values, lifestyle aspirations, and overall vision for your life.

What challenges or setbacks have I faced in life that have shaped my desire to build a business? How do these experiences fuel my motivation and resilience? Reflecting on personal challenges can help you uncover how past experiences are driving your entrepreneurial goals. Often, your why is rooted in your ability to overcome adversity and seek meaningful success.

If I could no longer run my business tomorrow, what would I feel I've left behind in the world? What legacy do I want to create through my work? This prompt helps you define your legacy and deeper contribution to the world, beyond financial success or daily operations. Your why often becomes clearer when you think about the lasting impact of your work.

I often recommend that founders and business owners return to their business's vision and mission statement once they've established their why, as it may have changed now that your motivations have changed too. From here, you're ready for the expansion practice.

Identifying Your Upper Limit Response

Before we can expand into something new, we need to know what our personal signs are that we're at our upper limit capacity to experience success. Personally, my tendencies are that I complain a lot and I have a part of me that's really skeptical of my success. It says things like "this won't last," "this isn't real," "somebody's tricking me," and "it's all going to go away."

Ask yourself in what ways do you notice yourself doubting, being skeptical of, or fighting success, ease, and abundance? You can reference the list below for ideas of self-sabotaging behaviors:

- procrastination
- perfectionism
- not following through on plans
- avoiding tasks that bring joy or fulfillment
- breaking up with or abandoning success when things go well

These are some physical and emotional responses:

- anxiety, stress, or physical discomfort (e.g., migraines, autoimmune issues)
- feeling unmotivated or apathetic
- detachment from goals or inspiration
- overwhelm leading to discontinuing progress

These are some signs you're avoiding abundance or joy:

- not setting or maintaining healthy boundaries
- hiding from or avoiding success
- postponing enjoyable activities or projects
- spending sprees or buying unnecessary things

These are ways to know you're staying in the comfort zone of scarcity:

- complaining or returning to insecurity
- always staying in research or planning phases without taking action
- feeling bored or uninspired after a leap in progress
- freezing or withdrawing after a significant success or identity shift
- making impulsive or reactive decisions
- making big changes or creating problems when things start going well

- making yourself invisible or not sharing your work when it's going well

Once you've identified your upper limit response from the list above, you're going to need something new to ground into. So take a moment to connect with your Self again. What does it feel like to experience success in your body? What does it feel like to experience groundedness in your body? What does it feel like to experience Self in your body? Specify one to three sensations, thoughts, or emotions.

For example, sensations might be heavy feet on the ground or breathing deep into the belly, thoughts might be *OMG, this feels good!* and emotions might be peace or groundedness. Last, in preparation for the expansion practice, you may need a new why.

The Expansion Practice

Here's how we do the expansion practice:

1. Identify your upper limit from this list above. When these patterns kick in, it's a sign you're expanding your capacity for success, pleasure, and ease. You're growing your ability to create impact without burning out—congratulations!

2. Instead of engaging in your old patterns, learn to "hold the pose" and expand in a new experience of success, ease, or pleasure—without trying to eliminate the worry or fear present. You'll hold this pose for seventeen seconds because this is usually enough time to shift out of your thinking mind and allow your body to feel safer experiencing more pleasure, ease, or success. This is exactly what that looks like:

    a. Orient to a sensation in your body that feels pleasurable, easy, satisfying, or successful and breathe your energy into it, focusing on it until it begins to feel more grounded and integrated in your body.

b. Bring your awareness to an emotion in your body, and allow it to be there.

c. Challenge yourself by finding a sensation or emotion that feels empowering and pleasurable to you and ask it to increase by 10 percent.

d. Hold that feeling for about seventeen seconds. Allow the fear or worry to be present, and continue holding the pose until the sensation neutralizes or your state changes. There will be times you feel euphoric and excited to move on, and sometimes you'll still feel pretty much the same. In the case of the latter, I recommend continuing with the practice, and also going back and looking at pillar 2 (trauma healing) to see if there is a part of you or a disempowering belief being triggered).

Debbie came up to me after class and said, "I realized I was doing all of this just to prove that I'm smart enough. It feels like how I used to feel when I had to prove it to my dad." She sat there for a moment, deflated, clearly sad about how hard she'd been working, pushing herself to prove something we all already knew—that she was smart enough. After sitting in that quiet, sad space for a bit, she mentioned wanting to identify her why but admitted she didn't know how.

I could sense a feeling of surrender in her. I encouraged her, just as I would encourage you, not to push the why. You don't have to figure it out right now. The why will come when it's ready. Allow yourself to be okay with not knowing. Plant the question in your mind, and your brain's natural curiosity—your RAS—will help you find the answer. There's no need to force it or prove that you know. Simply contemplate it, be open, and trust that it will arrive in its own time (plus, your RAS will help you focus on things that will answer the question).

On the other hand, you might be feeling more like Emily, who left that same workshop completely focused and clear on her why, her vision, and her legacy. She felt a fire within her and set a timer on her phone to practice expanding her nervous system capacity for seventeen seconds a day, avoiding self-sabotage. One Sunday morning not too long after, while resting, she looked up and saw the way that the sunlight touched on the plants and the bricks of the wall, sparkling like a little rainbow. Her whole body was filled with this space of ease, and she felt gratitude that, even though things had been so hard, she'd arrived at this place where she could lay with her partner by her side, watch the sun shining through the window and feel deeply happy and fulfilled. This feeling was priceless.

Now is a good time to highlight that neither Debbie nor Emily were doing things in a "better" way—they simply had different approaches. There will be moments when you move forward with fierce passion like Emily, and other times when you move more slowly (or what appears to be backward) like Debbie. Both are valid, both are healthy, and both will get you where you need to go—as long as you keep going.

Key Takeaways

- Actions and experiences such as worry, complaining, perfectionism, procrastination, or overspending stem from the nervous system's attempt to return to familiar states of insecurity or scarcity.
- The nervous system perceives sudden success or abundance as unfamiliar and potentially unsafe, triggering behaviors that pull individuals back to their previous baseline of scarcity or insecurity, even if it causes harm.

- By using regulation techniques such as grounding, creating safety, and reconnecting to a why, individuals can rewire their nervous system, gradually increasing their baseline capacity for connection, abundance, and success.

Now that you've started expanding your nervous system capacity for success, joy, and ease, you're ready to enter into pillar 3 of the BBB methodology and find the flow that allows you to share your work with the world.

Pillar 3:
Protocol

This pillar of the book represents something in your life that will either be a bed of nails or a perfect pillow-top, cushiony, memory-foam mattress perfectly shaped to your body that, as soon as you lie down, alleviates all the tension in your spine and makes you feel like you can sink into it and be deeply supported. We're talking about structures, which support your nervous system as it finds its way to more and more success, and help you get your work and vision out into the world.

Structures—the protocols and practical systems in our lives—can either make life harder, requiring constant regulation and healing, or they can support and uplift us, freeing up energy for what truly matters.

When I say structures, I'm referring to a range of things, from the personal habits you practice daily to larger systems like laws, social policies, or societal norms. While you have significant control over your personal structures, your influence over larger systems—such as laws, equity issues, or the patriarchy—is more limited. However, all of these structures impact your energy and capacity, and since every human has a finite amount of both, it's crucial to build supportive systems in your life.

These systems should feel like that perfect mattress, not a bed of nails, allowing you to focus your energy on tackling the bigger challenges in the world.

While our society has made progress, we're still navigating deeply flawed systems that cause great suffering to all of us. To create the radical change needed to provide sustainable futures and comfortable present moments, we need people like you to be financially comfortable, confident, creative, innovative, motivated, resilient, and inspired.

The world needs you to feel good in your work so that you can do more of it, better. When you feel good at work, your nervous system is supported, and when your version of success is aligned with your needs, you gain the capacity to create meaningful change.

This chapter is about setting up the foundational structures—your pillar of support—that will enable you to do good in the world. While you'll find practical guidance here for managing sales, marketing, team dynamics, client relationships, and your lifestyle, the ultimate intention is to help you define success on your own terms. Success doesn't have to feel rigid or out of reach; it can flow naturally from the essence inside you, from that tingling energy that starts deep within and moves through you from the tips of your toes to the point of your nose.

The next chapter will guide you in creating supportive systems that align with your unique definition of success. By doing so, you'll walk away with a sustainable path forward—one that empowers you to leave an impact, make meaningful changes, and feel truly successful in both your personal and professional life.

Chapter 13

Inspired Action

With Debbie and Emily both feeling more capacity for their purpose, pleasure, joy, and success, they found themselves shifting focus. Their thoughts were now less about how they could be successful or make money and more about how they could genuinely make an impact.

Debbie was thinking about offering workshops and training sessions for her clients on the importance of value-based branding and community building. Meanwhile, Emily had been invited to speak at a large conference about creating more equitable practices within the tech industry.

Debbie, however, kept telling herself she would take action once she felt more comfortable or after gathering more testimonials. She rationalized that there was a clear path forward but found herself spending a lot of time researching, listening to podcasts, and seeking opinions—essentially staying in a learning phase. Emily was caught in a similar loop, though it manifested differently. Her impostor syndrome crept back in, convincing her that her past success was a fluke and that she wouldn't be able to replicate it. She feared her audience wouldn't understand her evolving, more visionary ideas, and felt the weight of responsibility. Anxiety tightened her chest and shoulders, and a voice inside told her it was all about to fall apart.

What they didn't realize was that it was time to consciously integrate one of the most important parts of the Body-Based Business method: inspired action. The anxiety and uncertainty they were experiencing stemmed from falling into a common trap—not pairing their thinking, working, and processing with consistent, structured action that aligned with their unique mind, body, and goals.

When they arrived at class, they saw the following sentence on the projector: Success comes from inspired action, which leverages your somatic intelligence to create opportunities otherwise unavailable.

Many people get stuck because they want to feel comfortable before taking action. Like Debbie, they try to rationalize their way into certainty and calmness. It's futile and exhausting. Fear and apprehension are primal nervous system responses to uncertainty or threat—you can't outthink them. You can't logic your way into safety if your body hasn't experienced it yet.

However, when you take risky actions—whether it's asking for a sale, setting a boundary, speaking up, or creating a product your audience wants—your body starts to learn that it can work. It isn't as dangerous as it initially seemed, and over time, the fear dissolves, making future actions easier. But to be clear, you can't provide that safety for your nervous system without actually taking the action, which is why throughout this course, I've been encouraging just that. In this session, you'll learn to create more success externally and manifest your goals through structured, supported, and inspired action.

Feeling Safe Enough to Take the Leap

Now, I've been a little sneaky with you, holding off on sharing this until this point in the book. If I had introduced this concept earlier, as I used to when I began teaching it, it would have backfired. Without addressing your foundational nervous system responses, trauma, and limiting beliefs first, this idea could have felt overwhelming and unachievable. You might have even started taking more action, thinking it was inspired, when in reality, it could have been driven by fear or limiting beliefs. You might have gotten stuck trying to process everything in your head without the practice of being in a regulated nervous system, grounded in Self energy. That would have made it difficult to discern what true inspired action is and how to take it in a way that feels manageable.

Notice I say manageable, not easy. That's also why I waited until now—so you can continue using regulation and trauma healing while you add in manageable inspired action. Inspired action that is manageable isn't always easy. Later in this course, we'll dive into why success requires hard work, why pushing and challenging yourself is essential for fulfillment, resilience, and long-term success, and why we can't always take the easiest path—but we can take a more easeful one.

As I was sharing this, I noticed Emily deep in thought, taking notes and reflecting. Later, I found out she was thinking over the past year and recognizing how she'd applied this process. She took risks and acted before she was fully comfortable, and in doing so, she collected embodied evidence that the actions she took were safe. For example, she learned it was safe to stop micromanaging her employees, and as a result, they got their tasks done on their own, easing her concerns. She learned it was safe to experience more pleasure and ease, and with that, she no longer had to worry or be anxious as much as she had been when things got hard initially.

In contrast, Debbie, sitting next to her, started to feel a bit of regret for holding herself back and waiting to feel safe first. You could see the grimace on her face as she realized how much pain this had caused her.

It was clear she would need to do some emotional processing around her regret and gather the wisdom from it. If this resonates with you, take a moment to go back to your emotional alchemy practice and process any emotions that may come up as we continue through the chapter.

When we look at taking inspired action, it's important to return to regulation. If you're unable to regulate yourself in the face of discomfort, you're far more likely to avoid taking action altogether. But when you understand how to regulate your nervous system while stepping into the unknown, you create a foundation where it's safe to experiment, fail, and grow. This means you're more likely to succeed because you're not just pushing yourself through the fear; you're creating resilience in your body to navigate difficulty then return to a state of ease, groundedness, and pleasure. This teaches your body it can handle more challenges, allowing your RAS to present more opportunities that require growth and move you closer to your goals, even through periods of discomfort.

This is when we start to see how everything comes together: regulation, emotional processing, focus, beliefs, healing trauma, and taking action. However, in our search for safety around new actions, you must understand that you will never feel completely safe for most of the things you want to do in life. Instead of seeking absolute safety, aim for feeling *safe enough*. Complete safety is rarely achievable, especially if you have a female nervous system with more estrogen and generally lower physical strength than your testosterone driven counterparts. There's never enough security in the world to make your nervous system feel so safe it can completely relax—just like there's never enough money to feel completely secure. Even billionaires, like Elon Musk, have experienced moments when they had to borrow money despite their wealth.

As you move through this material, ask yourself these questions: *Am I safe enough to take this action? Am I safe enough to make this decision?* Don't wait for absolute certainty; recognize when you are safe enough to move forward. This even includes welcoming your skepticism.

Finding a Healthy Amount of Skepticism

When I talk about skepticism, I'm not saying you need to become some cynical detective who questions everything, like *What if the economy falls apart tomorrow?* Skepticism is another aspect of the quality of Self: curiosity. It's about allowing yourself to be patient, cautious, calm, and curious about all aspects of life. It's the part of you that thinks, *Hmm, okay, interesting… but let me just double-check before I jump in.* It's a safety mechanism, not a break in your progress.

There's nothing healthy about blind faith. If you've experienced religious or spiritual trauma, the concept of saying yes to something before you fully understand it might cause a visceral discomfort, and not only is that understandable, it's a sign you're integrating some wisdom from your past experiences.

Developing a healthy amount of skepticism will help you act on this wisdom from past experiences, and taking action with your skepticism present will stop you from getting stuck in loops of trying to convince your fear not to be there. Skepticism isn't about closing yourself off to possibility. Instead, it's about balancing healthy doubt with inspired action. You can counterbalance skepticism by using nervous system regulation, applying practical support systems, and adopting an attitude of experimentation.

Let's look at what a healthy amount of skepticism looks like in practice.

It's curious, not cynical.

Healthy skepticism asks questions like "How might this actually work for me?" instead of saying, "Ugh, this will never work." It's like the friend who's happy to road trip with you but insists on googling the gas station stops first—just in case.

It's open-minded but grounded.

It respects your past experiences (especially "oops, that didn't go as planned" moments) without locking you into a never-again mentality. Healthy skepticism leaves the door open for new outcomes while keeping an escape route handy.

It's proactive, not paralyzing.

It doesn't trap you in analysis paralysis. Instead, it nudges you to ask smart questions like "What can I do to make this feel less risky?" instead of saying, "I better not try because . . . yikes!"

It's protective, not limiting.

Think of it as a gentle guard dog—it'll bark to keep you safe from harm, but it doesn't bite everyone who walks by. It helps you pause and think before jumping in, but it doesn't hold you back from new opportunities.

It's open to evidence.

A healthy skeptic is happy to be proven wrong! It's here to experiment and learn, and honestly, it *wants* to be wrong (because that usually means things are going better than expected).

Real-Life Examples of Healthy Skepticism

- In business decisions, instead of declaring, "This strategy is definitely going to fail," you ask, "What's a small way I could test this without throwing everything at it?"
- In personal growth, instead of thinking *I can't trust myself ever again,* you might try *What small steps can I take to prove to myself that I've got this?*
- In sales and relationships, rather than jumping to conclusions like "This person won't be a good match for me," you ask, "How can I make sure we both get our needs met while we see if this partnership works?"

How to Balance Skepticism and Inspired Action

You can balance healthy skepticism with action by combining nervous system regulation, structure, and a willingness to experiment.

The first thing to do is regulate your nervous system.

Take a moment to ground yourself. Stand with your feet firmly planted, lift your heels slightly off the ground, and then gently tap them back down. Keep your jaw loose, your tongue soft (off the roof of your mouth), and your lips slightly parted. This simple exercise activates your parasympathetic nervous system, calming your body and creating a sense of safety.

Next, apply practical systems.

Set up clear performance metrics or project milestones that help you track progress and build confidence in the process. Knowing you have measurable steps in place creates a sense of control and safety.

Finally, you want to experiment and reflect.

Use an experimental mindset to move forward. Try something, write down what you did, and reflect regularly with questions like *What did I like about this experiment? What went well? What would I change in the future?*

This combination of regulation, structure, and reflection helps you bridge the gap between doubt and inspired action. You don't have to *feel* fully ready or convinced—it's about recognizing when you're safe enough to take the next step and then seeing your nervous system adapt and feel safer with those actions as you go. Each time you take action, even with fear and skepticism present, you create new neural pathways, reinforcing a safer narrative around what once felt threatening. Over time, you'll stop thinking *What if it goes wrong? What if I can't do this? What if they judge me?*

However, this works the other way too. If there's a genuine threat, it's irresponsible for anyone to suggest you can adjust your mindset to accommodate it or heal your way out of it. Be creative in finding ways to support yourself financially while still pursuing what matters to you. Financial stability is a form of self-care, and it's essential to ensure you achieve that first. Once your basic needs are met and you've addressed whether urgency comes from trauma (which we can heal) or a real threat (which we can work on solving), you can access inspired action that creates sustainable success.

The Compound Effect

Inspired action creates success because small, consistent steps add up over time—a principle known as the compound effect. It's like planting seeds: each action is a seed that, with time and care, grows into something meaningful. While it may not feel significant in the moment, the impact builds exponentially.

Here's how it works:

1. Regulation expands capacity. By regularly regulating your nervous system, you build resilience and expand your ability to handle challenges without burning out. Each time you face discomfort, take action, and return to balance, you're teaching your body that it's capable of navigating stress and uncertainty—which makes future actions feel less daunting.

2. Momentum builds. Each inspired action you take creates momentum. Early on, it might feel slow—like pushing a heavy boulder uphill—but over time, your actions make things easier, and progress starts to roll on its own. For example, reaching out to one potential client every day might not feel like much, but over a year, that's 365 opportunities. But this doesn't mean you need to do more! Pause and read to the end of the chapter before assuming so, please.

3. Confidence and growth compound. Every small win builds confidence and teaches your body that it can deal with scary or new things. As you take action and see progress, your RAS collects evidence that you can succeed. This creates a positive loop: action fuels belief, and belief fuels more action. Over time, your brain rewires itself to expect success, making inspired actions feel natural, exciting, or . . . even a little boring!

4. You get outstanding results. When I first started focusing more on inspired action, the results felt teeny-tiny until I was able to lie on my bed one day, having an absolutely awful day, feeling down and sorry for myself, and still see my business thriving. I thought about people asking me to speak on podcasts (something I'd dreamed of), building my income, and my work having a massive impact. I saw how every single small action had created the success and momentum of that one moment; I could see

outstanding results, independent of my emotional state that day or how much work I'd done that week. One call turns into a new client, which opens doors to more opportunities. Over months and years, this consistency creates a thriving and fulfilling business without needing to force, hustle or push—that's true sustainability and success.

This One Might Hurt

In the section above, I described the beauty of the compound effect and how it can work in your favor. However, it works the other way too.

What will your life look like if you don't take action and you stay exactly the same as you are now? If you continue to assume the worst and focus on negative thoughts like *It's not working* or *I can't do this*, you teach your brain to expect negative outcomes, creating a self-fulfilling prophecy. While you don't have to fully believe in the possibility of your desired reality from the start, you do need to practice embodying the belief that it's possible. Each step forward reinforces that belief, gradually rewiring your nervous system to support your new reality. But keep in mind, results take time due to the compound effect.

When You Want It All Now

If you're feeling impatient for results, recognize that urgency often stems from a dysregulated part of you that perceives danger in the delay. Perhaps a part of you is thinking that if you're not perfect or you don't figure this out now, nobody will love you. If that's the case, return to pillar 2: focus on unblending from that part and reconnecting to your regulated self. Alternatively, there may be a real threat, such as financial stress—money is running out and rent is due in three weeks. In this case, with love, I'd encourage you to get a job that requires less energy and provides your nervous system the stability it needs.

Forced Effort vs. Inspired Action

As I was teaching on the compound effect, I could see Emily—feeling inspired trying to hide the fact that she was already emailing her team a new to-do list. I could see Debbie start to get a little frustrated and overwhelmed. I could just imagine her thinking, *Great, you're just telling me to go out there and work harder. Cool, thanks!*

It took all my self-control not to grab that phone from Emily and tell her to breathe, pause, and wait. Instead, I affirmed to Debbie that, no, we wouldn't just be focusing on doing more or taking massive action, because, contrary to what so many business gurus teach you, doing more isn't the pathway to sustainable success.

Emily, excited and slightly anxious, came forward and interrupted, saying, "Well, I actually pushed myself really, really hard when I was working corporate, and it created the foundation for the success I'm having today. So effort and pushing definitely get results."

On one hand, she was right, and I told her so. However, I also called out a couple of points. Yes, forced effort and unrelenting hard work that ignores your physical, emotional, and spiritual needs will get you results, but it will also lead to burnout. Just picture that one guy a the office that will literally do all the work anyone asks him, is promoted often, and makes a whole bunch of money, but needs twelve cups of coffee a day, can't bear to be alone as he's chronically depressed, has a strained relationship with his wife and kids, and has heart issues at fifty-three.

Creating extraordinary success that doesn't compromise your physical and mental health or the quality of your relationships doesn't come from constant effort. It comes from inspiration, flow, and somatic intelligence. When you feel the urge to push so hard, it's often a sign that you're operating from a place of fear.

Emily paused and looked at me, so I asked if I could coach her a little. She nodded. I asked, "What might be uncomfortable about believing that you don't need to work and push so hard to find success?" She took a deep breath, swallowed, and I could see something was caught in her throat. Tears welled in her eyes as she realized the answer: she would have to admit that she had worked so hard, hurt herself, depleted herself, and damaged relationships when she hadn't needed to. She had been so hard on herself, causing immense emotional pain and turmoil. All that time, she hadn't needed to rush or prove anything. It was sad for her to realize how much energy she had wasted doing it, and it was something she would need to grieve.

Immediately, she felt compassion for herself. This is something many high achievers experience—we realize we've been working so hard, and while it has been helpful in some ways, it's also caused a lot of discomfort and damage. Often, this urge to push, struggle, and exert our way to success stems from a belief picked up in childhood—a need to prove ourselves or the feeling that we can't trust what's inside of us. It brings us to bigger questions: Can you trust yourself? What would you do if you could trust yourself?

Taking inspired action requires believing that you can trust the somatic intelligence inside of you. Most of society is set up to teach us that we can't trust our own life force energy. Somatic intelligence, or body-based wisdom, is innate to everyone, yet many of us have learned that we can't trust this energy. It might be helpful for you to remember at this point that somatic intelligence is our optimal path toward satisfaction and feelings of success, peace, ease, and excitement in life.

Just like healthy cells perform their individual jobs to help the entire body function at its best capacity, individuals can access that same intelligence to perform their individual jobs to support their own well-being, and that of our communities, in the most effortless and seamless way.

As individuals, we can use somatic intelligence to help us reach optimal performance and peace, which helps us give back to the community and work together with more harmony. In today's world, this approach might seem far-fetched, taboo, and even dangerous to others. That's why society at large often teaches us to do what others think we should do, and this disconnect from our own energy leaves us feeling depleted.

Inspired action comes from trusting your somatic intelligence and analytical skills (such as logical reasoning, problem-solving, risk evaluation, and critical thinking) to navigate the world we live in today. For those who are spiritually connected, this might also involve trusting in what Spirit, God, or the Divine wants you to do in this world. Somatic intelligence and inspired action won't ask you to push through exhaustion because you feel like you should, but they may inspire you to work hard because you genuinely want to.

Inspired action might be the nudge that tells you to reach out to a colleague who mentions a workshop they're hosting. You attend, connect with someone passionate about your vision, and they offer to partner with you to create the curriculum you've been dreaming of—helping you expand your impact in ways you hadn't imagined. It's your access point to synchronicities, resilience, and creating a sustainable business aligned with your needs and the larger community's needs.

EXERCISE: Accessing Inspired Action

Okay, so now that we know why inspired action is so important, let's look at how to do it .

Step 1: Anchor and embody one or both of these options.

- Option 1: Bring to mind one of the new, empowering beliefs you're working on, such as one of these:
  o Following our somatic intelligence creates a pathway for us to find our unique place in the world.
  o This business can and will work (a belief I've had to practice a lot!)
  o I cannot fail, and even if I feel like I do, I'm loved and safe.
  o People want to hear my unique perspective.
  o I can trust myself, and I know what I'm doing.
- Option 2: Pop back to chapter 12 and use the expansion practice to access a feeling of well-being and success.

Step 2: As you embody one of the new, empowering beliefs or access a sensation of well-being, ask the question (or a variation that feels right for you) "What is the next natural action to take, knowing this is safe and true?"

Step 3: Pause and wait until you get an answer from a felt sense, a thought, or an urge to take a specific action.

Step 4: Wait. Receiving an answer could take half a second or it might take a few weeks, or even months. I encourage staying still and silent for up to thirty minutes waiting for a response. If it hasn't come after that, you can either continue about your life until it does come or consider returning to pillars 1 and 2 and using regulation and somatic parts work or emotional alchemy to make space for a new answer to come forward. If it's really just not coming to you, consider reaching out for one-to-one support to help you move past your thoughts into the body and toward your somatic intelligence. The answer is there—sometimes it's just harder to see and we need someone else to help us shine a light to find it.

Step 5: Take the action as soon as you can do so in a grounded way. Experiment and gather information. This is not about getting things right; it's about learning about yourself and the world.

Step 6: After some time has passed (you'll either know how long this needs to be naturally, or you can pick a time period of your choice), reflect. Consider what you learned about yourself, your decision, and others through your experience. Here are some questions to ask yourself as you reflect:

- What felt really good about this action?
- What didn't feel great?
- What would you like to repeat and experience more of?
- What would you change if you did it again?

Debbie sat and listened to all of this, realizing that she had been trying to logic her way through the fear. She decided to take inspired action. She reached out to a friend who supports people in creating courses and educational content, and within the next month, she had something up and ready to sell.

Emily also found her version of inspired action. When she anchored into the inspired action exercise, she felt an expansive sense of "I can do this." In fact, she thought, *I can do this more, and I can do this better.* She messaged her colleagues and asked if she could contribute to their new program as an educator on social justice and workplace equality in tech. They offered her a generous sum for her support, and she began applying what she called "conscious marketing" to this new group.

Your version of inspired action will be unique, and it's exciting to see how it plays out and evolves in different moments of your life.

Key Takeaways

- Inspired actions are created when you pull from somatic intelligence and all your intellect and logic to create new opportunities in the way that is easier for you. This creates an upward spiral of growth.
- Regulating your nervous system allows you to take risks without waiting to feel completely safe, helping you build resilience and continue moving forward even in discomfort.
- Your body may resist new beliefs and ways of being in the world; however, through repeated small leaps of faith, you train your nervous system to adapt and create new, supportive neural pathways for success.

Now that you've started taking inspired action, you're ready to find true nervous system resilience so that your entrepreneurial career becomes more sustainable and feels like you're flowing through it (instead of hustling and pushing).

Chapter 14

The Keys to Sustainable Entrepreneurship

Debbie had returned to her nervous system regulation and was moving forward, but she still felt like she was struggling. It seemed like she was trying to be responsible for everything, leaving her scattered throughout her day. She noticed things were slipping through the cracks. When she went to her therapist, she often felt overwhelmed with emotion and would leave the session feeling heavy, like there was too much to hold. Despite all her efforts to regulate and do the work, it felt like things were falling apart. People even started coming forward, pointing out that deliverables were missing or details were out of place. Debbie wanted to feel like she was flowing through challenges, staying on track, and focusing on work amid the chaos. Most of all, she wanted to rely on her work and trust in herself.

Emily, while not as scattered, still resonated with the desire to feel things flowing more smoothly. She was spending a lot of time celebrating her new changes, and had gone eight months without a migraine. Even though her advocacy work was challenging, she was using her tools and working through her emotions. Things were going well, but still, there was something missing.

Both Debbie and Emily were noticing that, although they were embracing their challenges, they didn't feel truly resilient. It seemed to take them longer than they'd like to bounce back from setbacks. They began projecting forward, wondering how they would keep this pace up for the next ten years. Debbie, feeling overwhelmed, even started looking at traditional jobs, thinking owning her own business might all be too much. Emily, meanwhile, was thinking about how she would manage if she decided to have another child. Creatively, emotionally, and intellectually, she questioned how she could sustain this energy forever.

Working at the pace and with the attitudes they had been up until now had felt necessary because their trauma had been driving them—pushing them to prove themselves, to keep going, to stay in motion. But now that motivation was starting to wane, especially when it came to the more mundane tasks. Emily felt like her body just couldn't do it, even though she knew it was important, made sense, and earned her money. She was confused because she had always felt inspired—she was the one who always had energy when others didn't and was able to keep going. What neither of them realized was that they had been missing a key part of sustainable entrepreneurship: resilience.

When they arrived at that day's session, Emily saw the words *resilience* and *flow* on the projector and wanted to leave. It sounded like something she'd heard before. However, she trusted the process, knowing every other part of the course had helped, so she stayed—and learned it wasn't at all like what she had heard before. Let's start with definitions.

Flow is that magical state where you're so absorbed in what you're doing that time seems to disappear. Studies show that accessing your flow state enhances performance and improves your creativity and well-being.[19]

For me, cultivating flow has been one of the reasons I've stayed excited about my business for over a decade. At first, I protected that flow state simply because it felt good. Later, I realized that I was naturally creating the conditions for flow, and that was why I was able to stay engaged and motivated in my work for so long. Flow, I believe, is the true key to resilience.

Most people think resilience means grit, force, or ruthlessness, but it's really about finding flow and ease through and after challenges—not just getting things done. In fact, the buzz around nervous system regulation is really about nervous system *resilience*—and that's exactly what you've been learning.

Resilience is the ability to bounce back from challenges effectively and efficiently. You know you're more resilient when it takes you ninety seconds to recover from a tough email instead of the three days it used to take you.

When we are resilient and operating from somatic intelligence, we naturally experience more consistent states of flow. We've been practicing resilience through nervous system regulation and trauma healing (pillars 1 and 2). Now, it's time to work backward from the goal and find resilience

19. David J. Harris, Kate L. Allen, Samuel J. Vine, and Mark R. Wilson, "A systematic review and meta-analysis of the relationship between flow states and performance," *International Review of Sport and Exercise Psychology 16*, no. 1 (2023), https://doi.org/10.1080/1750984X.2021.1929402; Nicola S. Schutte and John M. Malouff, "Connections between curiosity, flow and creativity," *Personality and Individual Differences 152* (2020): 109555, https://doi.org/10.1016/j.paid.2019.109555; Remus Ilies, David Wagner, Kelly Wilson, Lucia Ceja, Michael Johnson, Scott DeRue, and Dan Ilgen, "Flow at Work and Basic Psychological Needs: Effects on Well-Being," *Applied Psychology 66*, no. 1 (2016): 3–24, https://doi.org/10.1111/apps.12075.

by finding more flow. They both influence, feed, and increase each other. Let's break that down.

Sustainable entrepreneurship is about your ability to access flow more frequently and over a longer period of time. Flow provides the sense of fulfillment that keeps you engaged and

motivated to move forward. It's also a signpost that your somatic intelligence is being expressed—when your body is expressing its intelligence, work gives you energy—it doesn't drain you. Finding flow means finding somatic intelligence, which is a way to ensure you have the energetic capacity for the work you're doing. This balance allows you to sustain your efforts without burning out.

How to Access Flow and Be More Resilient

Both resilience and flow happen when you're engaged in something that challenges you just enough to stretch your skills but not so much that it frustrates or overwhelms you.

If every action you take is too big or too overwhelming, you're going to burn out. On the flip side, if the challenges you take on are too small or easy, you'll get bored and disengage. Neither extreme will activate the areas of your brain that cultivate flow.

This delicate balance keeps you motivated, engaged, and productive. On a nervous system level, you'll experience slight levels of activation but not a full-on stress response.

Flow will look and feel like a balance between calm and focus.

- You focus effortlessly. Distractions fall away, and you're fully immersed. Time may feel like it's slowing down or speeding up, depending on the task, because your brain's ability to track time becomes less relevant.

- You experience heightened energy without tension. You might notice a surge of energy, but unlike stress-induced adrenaline, this energy is smooth and not frantic. Your heart rate may increase slightly, but it's steady, not chaotic, and your breathing is deep and rhythmic.

- Body awareness fades. Physical discomfort or awareness of your body tends to diminish as your brain devotes resources to the task. You may not notice hunger, fatigue, or even minor pain until after you've exited the flow state.

- You have clear, calm confidence. There's a sense of knowing exactly what to do next. You feel highly competent, and doubt doesn't creep in. Your nervous system is in a state of balance—alert yet calm.

- Dopamine release gives you a sense of pleasure. Dopamine is a neurotransmitter that plays a key role in reward, motivation, and pleasure in the brain. In flow state, it rewards your brain for staying on task and you feel good.

- Some people report a light, almost buzzing sensation in their bodies when deeply in flow, as though energy is moving freely without being impeded. This can feel like warmth or a pleasant hum under the skin.

- Your movements become relaxed and fluid. If you're moving, such as in athletic or creative activities, your motions become more graceful and efficient. Muscle tension decreases, and your actions feel smooth and synchronized.

Optimal Flow Conditions

At this point, I'll clear up a common myth about the nervous system: not all dysregulation is bad. The truth is, we need a certain amount of stress and pressure to feel fulfillment. If your business is always easy and predictable, you'll feel bored and detached. You need challenges to keep yourself engaged. It's the same reason why constriction and release create excitement in other areas of life. Think about the dynamics of physical exercise or even sex—there's a balance between tension and release that creates excitement and fulfillment. This same dynamic exists in entrepreneurship.

If you're constantly bored in your business, it's likely because you aren't challenging yourself enough. On the other hand, if you're constantly stressed out, you're probably overchallenging yourself. The key is to find that sweet spot. You need to find the right level of challenge.

It's simple to think about when we compare it to working out and building muscle. In order for muscles to grow stronger, they need to be torn just a little. But if you tear them too much, you injure yourself. Similarly, you want to take on challenges that stretch you just enough to build resilience, but not so much that you overwhelm your nervous system.

In your business, this might look like choosing actions that are slightly outside your comfort zone but still attainable. You want to feel that bit of pressure, that sense of "I'm not sure I can do this" because that's where growth happens. But you also need to regulate yourself before, during, and afterward. When the challenge is over, take the time to ground and restore your nervous system, so you don't stay in a perpetual state of stress.

These are the optimal conditions for flow[20]:

1. A challenge-skill balance (the demands of the activity match with one's ability).
2. Clear goals.
3. A clear way to see that your efforts have achieved something. For example:
    - Your new marketing campaign boosted traffic by 40 percent— proof it's working.
    - You meditate daily; anxiety levels drop and you feel calmer.
    - Your partner says, "When you listened, I felt heard." Clear cause and effect.

Flow state is a natural state of life when you follow your somatic intelligence. The reason you don't experience it as much as you'd like to is because you're experiencing common barriers to flow.

- Studies show that the inner critic is one of the biggest barriers to achieving flow. By using the practices inside pillar 2 of the BBB method, you'll be able to calm your inner critic and access flow more easily.
- You may have resistance to goal setting. Trauma related to goal setting can make it difficult to embrace clear goals, which are essential for flow. If you have stress or fear of failure around setting goals, I recommend using the practices in pillar 2 to heal and open yourself up to working with goals more effectively.
- You lack clear goals or direction. Flow thrives on clarity. Without specific goals, you might feel lost or unfocused, leading to frustration and disruption of your ability to concentrate. Ground

20. David J. Harris, Kate L. Allen, Samuel J. Vine, and Mark R. Wilson, "A systematic review and meta-analysis of the relationship between flow states and performance," *International Review of Sport and Exercise Psychology 16*, no. 1 (2023), https://doi.org/10.1080/175098 4X.2021.1929402.

yourself in your why, as identified in chapter 12, to create a deeper sense of direction and purpose in your work.

- Feedback is traumatic for you. Just like goal setting, feedback is another key component of flow. If receiving feedback triggers stress or fear of failure, the pillar 2 practices can help you heal this trauma and allow feedback to support your growth and flow.

- You experience dysregulation, stress, and anxiety. When your nervous system is in a state of high alert, it becomes challenging to focus or engage with tasks. Stress activates the fight-or-flight response, which diverts energy away from creativity and problem-solving, making flow difficult to access. Use the stress-management practices in pillar 2 to bring yourself back into regulation and flow.

- One of the biggest barriers to accessing flow state is actually being interrupted. I like to think of the nervous system when it's committed to focusing on something as similar to a hunter tracking a squirrel in the wilderness. In order to catch that squirrel, it needs to tune out everything irrelevant. This is why, when we're deeply focused on a task and someone tries to get our attention, we get so frustrated and annoyed—it pulls us out of that flow, and it can be really hard to refocus.

We can use this understanding of what stops us from accessing flow state to actually help us access more flow. In fact, we'll do this in a five-step process.

EXERCISE: Creating Flow State

Step 1: Reduce the Barriers to Flow

To start, ask yourself *What does my inner critic need to rest and relax? How can I quiet the criticism I feel when working or reflecting on my work?* I recommend returning to pillar 2 to dialogue with your inner critic, learning how to care for it, love it, and support it, so that it doesn't need to shut down your creativity.

Next, examine your fear of failure. What do your inner parts need in order to feel safe? How can you hold the pose of compassion, care, and self-love inside your body, so that fear of failure becomes a sensation you experience and gently release, rather than something that overwhelms you? Pillar 2 will help you with this as well. The same approach can be applied to any trauma around feedback—practice regulation and resourcing yourself with care, compassion, and love when receiving feedback.

Additionally, address dysregulation, stress, and anxiety. What practices, tools, and systems help you become more regulated? For me, this means scheduling a breathwork session at least once a month and being mindful of how I speak to myself during stressful moments. Sometimes I need to release expectations of myself, which ironically helps me achieve more. Reflect on what helps you stay regulated and manage stress effectively.

Another essential step is gaining clarity. Work with a friend, mentor, or coach to clarify your goals. Revisit your why, your vision, and your mission. What do you want to achieve? Are your goals coming from a place of care, devotion, and a genuine desire to contribute? Or are they rooted in fear, and you're trying to control or manipulate outcomes? Once you've clarified your goals and reduced the barriers to flow, you can move to the next step.

Step Two: Choose Your Skill and Your Task

We will use the stress scale developed by Deb Dana to guide this process.[21]

---

21. Deb Dana, *Anchored: How to Befriend Your Nervous System Using Polyvagal Theory* (Sounds True, 2021).

On this stress scale, you can see that on the right side, we have what happens to the nervous system when you push it too far into a difficult challenge. When the challenge feels much bigger than your perceived capacity, your nervous system enters a stress state. A dysregulated nervous system lives here—this is where anxiety kicks in, tension rises, and avoidance takes over. This happens when a task feels too overwhelming or uncertain, or when you don't believe in your ability to handle it. Remember, this is all about perception, not necessarily reality. The further past difficult the challenge goes, the further right you'll slide on the scale until you find yourself in the survive state.

In the middle of the scale, we have the neutral zone, where there isn't much of a nervous system response. This is where things feel pretty neutral and sometimes even boring. While this can be a comforting place, especially if other areas of your life are more difficult, it's not where flow state typically happens. That said, neutral tasks can be made more engaging. For example, if you have to do mundane admin work, you can put on a podcast or some interesting music to make it more challenging for your brain, bringing you closer to a flow state.

For flow, we want to be closer to the stretch side of the scale. This is where the task is challenging enough to engage your nervous system but not so difficult that it causes dysregulation. This is the sweet spot, where you feel a slight activation—just enough to stretch you, to make you focus, and to help you blur out distractions. It's like your primal body recognizes a challenge, focuses on it as a manageable threat, and blocks everything else out to get the job done. This is the place where flow happens.

Take a moment to think about the tasks in your life.

- What are the tasks that dysregulate you? For many, these involve interacting with others—like sales, difficult conversations, or, in my case, writing this book. That was dysregulating at first because I worried about what you might think. Thankfully, you've learned a whole methodology on how to manage that!
- What tasks are neutral for you and would put you in the middle of the scale? For me, this is usually tasks like accounting, sending emails, or other admin work that feels dull and uninspiring.
- Now, what tasks are a little challenging and move you toward a stretch? These should be challenging but enjoyable, allowing you to stretch and savor the process. For me, that might be writing or speaking, and perhaps for Emily, it's creating content or giving a presentation. These are the tasks where we can stretch ourselves just enough to access that yummy flow state.

Step Three: Set Your SMART Goal

Once you have your task, the next step is to set a goal. I like to use the SMART goal framework for this. It's nothing groundbreaking—you've probably heard of it before. I actually ignored it for a while because a rebellious part of me thought, *No! I learned about this in high school. I'll never do it again.* But I came back to it because, honestly, it works.

Here's how SMART goals work:

1. **Specific**—your goal should be clear and specific.

Example: Publish one podcast.

2. **Measurable**—you should be able to measure your progress.

Example: I want to publish two podcasts per week.

3. **Actionable**—ensure the goal is something you can take action on.

Example: Yes, I can take action by recording and editing the podcast.

4. **Relevant**—the goal should be relevant to your larger objectives.

Example: This goal is relevant to my business, especially if I include a call to action in each episode to either listen to another podcast or inquire about my self-assessment programs.

5. **Time-bound**—set a time frame for achieving the goal.

Example: I will record the podcast next Thursday between 2:00 and 4:00 p.m. To make it easier, set this as a recurring task. You might decide to record every Thursday from 2:00 to 4:00 p.m. for the next six weeks.

At the end of six weeks, you can reflect on what you've learned from setting and working toward this goal, then make any necessary modifications.

Step Four: Get Unambiguous Feedback

Ugh, this is the part I hate. My fear of not being smart enough comes out to play, putting tension in my chest and making me want to run for the hills. However, it's essential for success and necessary if you want to create anything of value, for anyone, ever—except for the times it's not. See, this is where the science tells you to do something, and maybe it's the inner rebel in me or maybe it's intelligence—who knows—I disagree. I don't think it's as simple as that. There are two sides to this. First, you could look for direct feedback, but if you're like me and have a deep fear of not being smart enough, a large part of taking a body-based approach to business is recognizing, acknowledging, and even appreciating your fears. So, if you have something inside of you saying *Ugh, this is hard and sticky*, it doesn't mean you need to heal everything before moving forward. Instead, it means you can acknowledge that something is difficult for you and find other ways to approach it.

In business, feedback is always occurring. Your business is constantly giving you feedback. For example, if revenue is down, that's feedback. If employee engagement is up or your team is happy, that's also feedback. If you approach it from a place of regulation, you can interpret it and figure things out. So, yes, the science says clear and immediate feedback allows you to adjust your actions in real time and stay on track, but be creative about how you interpret this. Find a method that works for you.

For me, I enjoy self-reflection: *What felt good in my body? What would I change next time?* Some people thrive off input from others, asking "What do you see that I could have done differently?" Or maybe you build a sense of community and connection by involving your team or clients, especially if you thrive on helping others. The point is to get feedback in a way that feels natural and doesn't create stress or anxiety.

Step Five: Use Rituals to Ground and Restore Yourself

A resilient nervous system and resilient entrepreneurship involve consistently returning to a sense of ease. Throughout the day, we should be coming back to moments of ease, softness, connection, laughter, and play. These moments of ease are essential, especially around high-pressure situations like work sprints, difficult conversations, or stepping out of your comfort zone. But it's just as important to cultivate ease when things are going well.

When I say "ritualize," I mean creating repetitive and predictable actions—small routines that your body automatically does. These actions send a signal to your nervous system that it's safe, helping you shift into a new part of your day. Rituals access the deeper parts of your psyche, a wisdom humans have understood since the beginning of ritual practice. They support deeper focus, productivity, and a profound sense of well-being.

For example, if you know that taking a walk helps you access flow, schedule it into your day. Don't wait until you're exhausted—make it a regular part of your routine. Or, if you experience emotional ups and downs, recognize that as part of your personality. I know that whenever I make a decision, I feel a range of emotions: excitement, fear, sadness, disappointment, excitement again, and finally, neutrality. I let the people in my life know this, so we all understand what to expect, and I make sure decision-making is a process, not something rushed. Perhaps you do something similar, like scheduling meetings during times when your energy is higher and allowing for downtime when you need it.

This is all about creating routines and systems that increase your well-being. Studies show that people who regularly experience flow are less susceptible to depression,[22] and I believe it's important for you—and everyone around you—to experience more well-being and less depression. This is how we create a world we enjoy living in, and it's how we build businesses that contribute positively to that world.

---

22. Emma Gaston, Fredrik Ullén, Laura W. Wesseldijk, and Miriam A. Mosing, "Can flow proneness be protective against mental and cardiovascular health problems? A genetically informed prospective cohort study," *Translational Psychiatry 14*, no. 144 (2024), https://doi.org/10.1038/s41398-024-02855-6.

The premise of this whole approach, and why I'm teaching you to access more flow, is that when you do so consistently, everything starts to feel like it's flowing. You begin to see synchronicities, and the entire process of building your business becomes fun. Let's be honest—there are countless ways you could spend your time and energy, so you deserve to be doing something that is enjoyable in the process. There's no need to delay gratification or burn yourself out to reach a goal. Making the process flowy and fun—*that* is success. *That* is resilience. And *that* is how you create impact, prevent burnout, and build a sustainable business.

Debbie sat and listened, and I swear I could feel those last few words really resonating with her. So, I was a little surprised when, a couple of weeks later, we reconnected, and she told me she hadn't really resonated with the idea of flow. Instead, she had been pushing through, just doing all the things. Part of me could see that she needed to neutralize her inner critic a bit more. She hadn't been able to access flow because that inner voice was telling her *You have to get this done now. You haven't done enough. You can't take a walk. You're doing it wrong.* I could sense a palpable fear of failure—she was very concerned about getting everything right and hitting her goals now.

The tension she felt was building, and the time she spent in a fight response was ramping up. She was worried about what might happen if she didn't succeed and didn't reach a certain income in six months. And because of that, she hadn't yet connected with a healthy sense of why. While she had been making some progress, the journey felt long. But I was happy knowing that in our next session, we could at least support and bolster her to access more flow and resilience.

Emily, of course, had a different approach. With her fiery mind, she took her SMART goals and ran with them. She aimed to secure three new partnerships by the end of the quarter. While she didn't get all three, she managed to land two. She even put a picture of the stress scale up next to her desk to remind herself to stay in that sweet spot—the stress-savor place. She used somatic check-ins throughout the day, asking herself simple questions like *How alert am I? How focused am I?* This helped her feel and sense where she was along the scale.

However, Emily was noticing another challenge. Whenever she committed to getting something done, her partner or child would come up and try to get her attention. She would find herself getting really frustrated and then feeling guilty for not being a good spouse or mother. What I suggested to her was to protect that focused state more consciously.

It's important to understand that when your body and brain are locked in on a task, it's natural for them not to be able to shift attention easily. The energy is funneled toward "catching the squirrel"—whether that's writing the book, solving a problem, or creating something. This is a normal, natural response. The best thing you can do is set your environment and life up to minimize distractions and interruptions.

For Emily, I recommended establishing something like team time. This means setting clear boundaries, such as saying "Between these hours, I'm focused. You can check in with me at midday, but hold all your questions until then." This creates space for focus while also providing designated times for connection and responsiveness.

Emily also implemented a morning walk before tackling any of her leadership tasks. This became a nonnegotiable ritual, helping her calm her nervous system and create a sense of predictability and safety. It set her up to carry that focus and connection with her deeper why into the rest of her day. At the end of each day, she spent ten minutes doing a brain dump into her journal, which helped her disconnect from work and transition into time with her partner and child.

Because of these actions, Emily experienced more peace. She slept better, felt more successful, and found joy in watching her child thrive at school and in family life. She felt proud of who she had become, and others could feel it too. People began asking her "How did you do it? What's your secret? You're so magnetic, so radiant!" It brought her a lot of pleasure to see the way others responded to her transformation.

You'll be able to access that same radiance and magnetism. People will become excited to be around you, to follow your lead. They'll want to know your secret. I experienced this myself, and it's what led to the creation of the BBB methodology. People asked me "How did you do this?" And when I'm fully aligned with the methodology—because I'm human, I sometimes fall off—I notice it too. People are drawn in. They want to be part of what I'm doing. Let's get you to that same place.

Key Takeaways

- Resilience in entrepreneurship isn't about constant struggle but about bouncing back from challenges, cultivating a balance between challenge and ease.
- Accessing the flow state consistently enhances resilience, creativity, and performance by balancing tasks that are challenging but not overwhelming.
- Sustainable success requires building self-leadership protocols, setting clear goals, managing feedback, and grounding the nervous system to maintain flow and avoid burnout.
- Now that you've accessed your flow state, you're ready to set up protocols that will help you spend less time regulating, healing, and thinking, and more time enjoying your life and making the world a better place.

Chapter 15
Protocols for Success

Debbie and Emily both felt like they were swimming against the tide. Debbie was working harder, but it felt like she was constantly battling her inner critic, never able to stop. She had tried regulation and emotional healing, but the way her clients were speaking to her, the financial impact of her divorce, and the needs of her child were all pressing against her. It felt like she just couldn't get ahead.

Emily, on the other hand, had a bit of a spring in her step. She felt energized and happy, and she had taken on a big project that encapsulated her mission to empower companies to prioritize mental health. However, she was starting to feel a bit deflated because, despite her suggestions for impactful changes, she was struggling to implement all the changes she wanted because they went against current policies and norms within her social systems and laws.

In this chapter we'll be focusing on implementing personal and professional protocols that will help you and your teams create structures that naturally support well-being and productivity so that you can free up energy to address larger systemic challenges effectively.

When it comes to sustainable change, while regulation and self-leadership can create incredible change, operating within a system or structure that is actively working against us takes a lot of energy and we become less effective. However, when we can use our energy to create systems, relationships, containers, and protocols that naturally support us being in flow and regulation, we're able to do really wonderful things in the world. Ultimately, this is how we address larger issues like gender equality or lack of access to clean water.

When Debbie and Emily arrived at class and we had our initial sharing circle, it became clear that now was the time to talk about how success is really created. I sat down and began to teach how protocols influence success. If we're honest, success on your own terms requires building regulation and flow into every protocol you have throughout the day. This includes the self-leadership we've been studying, as well as administrative and leadership protocols that support you and your business mission in the world.

When we use these systems, structures, and protocols to support our own flow state, we not only shape our own energy but also influence the community around us to innovate, be creative, stay persistent, and act courageously in pursuit of the change we seek in the world. At the same time, we model what it looks like to be a regulated, empowered, and effective individual.

This chapter is going to give you tangible examples of how to do this, and I'm going to encourage you to act on them, regardless of the emotional state you might be feeling in the moment. These protocols and systems create a structure that makes your body feel safe because they provide predictability. We know that your nervous system craves predictability, safety, and security, and when we reduce decision-making, we gain access to flow.

I'm not suggesting you repress your emotions while implementing these systems, but rather that you validate, acknowledge, and make a note to create space for them at another time when you can alchemize them. As we learned in pillar 2, emotions and the body send stories that create thoughts that are not the full objective truth from a grounded perspective. By acknowledging the emotions, enacting the protocol, and then returning to alchemize the emotion—or alchemizing the emotion and then continuing with inspired action within a protocol—you have the safety and support set up to support you, your vision, and your business.

By integrating these protocols and examples, you'll experience the following:

- Increased decision-making capacity, especially under pressure
- Integrated creative, logical, and intuitive thinking to produce results that would otherwise be unattainable through traditional planning or strategy
- Access to inspired action and the ability to achieve success while maintaining emotional balance
- Reduced overwhelm and anxiety
- The ability to handle the uncertainty of sales and marketing
- The ability to navigate conflict with grace and ease
- The ability to build a healthy team environment
- The ability to manage client relationships with clear boundaries while fostering trust
- The ability to balance authentic self-expression in marketing without succumbing to social media burnout

Before diving into all of the suggested protocols, remember you have permission to skim. Focus only on what feels applicable to you at this moment. Not everything has to be done at once.

Addressing Barriers to Protocols

Let's go over some common barriers that might stop you from implementing these protocols and what you can do to overcome them.

Barrier 1: Feeling overwhelmed by structure

If reading about protocols and systems makes you tense or resistant, it might be because of past experiences when structure was imposed on you in a way that felt stifling or overwhelming. You might have felt like you didn't have a choice or control.

Go back to pillar 2 to reflect upon and notice your response to structure. This could be an opportunity to heal a past experience when expectations were placed on you and you felt powerless to say no.

Unlike in childhood, now you have the power and agency to create and change structures. Remind yourself that you get to choose what works for you. There's no authoritative figure dictating how you must operate.

Healing past trauma around structure comes from realizing that today, you have agency—you have a choice. You can adapt or change systems if they don't serve you.

Barrier 2: A perfectionist mindset

If you find yourself worried about "getting this right," or even procrastinating because you're not sure how or where to start, you might be putting a lot of pressure on yourself to be perfect. The solution to a perfectionist mindset is to adopt an experimental mindset so that you can come from a place of curiosity. In practice, this could look like experimentation, gamification, and making small changes.

Pick one protocol to try for a week, and then check in with yourself. Decide if your experiment worked or if it needs tweaking.

Make it a game. What can you learn from the experiment? How can you make this process fun?

Communicate the experiment by letting the people around you know you're experimenting. You could say something like "Hey, I'm trying out this new schedule. I might stick with it, but I also might decide to change it."

There's no need for a complete overhaul. Choose one aspect of your routine to change and experiment with at a time.

Barrier 3: Overstructuring

Perhaps you like organization, and you try to perfect every system and structure. While structure is valuable, too much of it can kill spontaneity, which is essential for inspired action.

Build time for spontaneity into your system. For instance, schedule extra time in your day or create space to do something unexpected.

Try some protocols for spontaneity. If you're driven by lists and goals, add tasks like ordering a different coffee, taking a new route to work, or engaging differently with a client.

Teach your body it's safe. By gradually doing more spontaneous things, you teach your nervous system that it's safe to step outside your usual routines, creating more room for creativity and success.

Barrier 4: Procrastination in the name of systems

Sometimes, creating elaborate systems becomes a way to avoid doing the actual work. The truth is, we're never avoiding a task itself—we're avoiding the emotions and sensations that come with that task.

Recognize procrastination disguised as planning. If you find yourself endlessly organizing instead of completing the work, notice if you're using systems as a way to avoid vulnerability or discomfort.

Build iteration periods. Create a system in which you allow yourself to release a project and then go back to refine it later. For example, make your website live but schedule a time to update or change it a week later. This gives your brain a sense of safety, knowing that adjustments can be made after the fact.

Give yourself permission to change. Let yourself release perfectionism by allowing changes and adaptations after trying something.

Example Categories of Protocols

I've found it to be helpful to divide protocols up into five sections: self-leadership, time management, administrative management, sales and marketing, and relationship management. Below you'll find examples for each one that will help you use the BBB method to increase the amount of time you spend in flow state, become more creative, and create success that honors your body and values.

Self-Leadership

Self-leadership focuses on personal emotional intelligence, time management, health, and mindset. This is where the Body Based Business strategy comes into play, allowing you to develop emotional resilience and effective decision-making skills.

Protocol 1: Use the BBB method.

Even as the creator of this methodology, I often forget or feel resistance to using it, despite knowing that each time I do, I feel better, treat others better, and get things done. The first protocol is simply committing to use the method regularly. To help, I've created a simple checklist that you can use when facing a challenge, recurring thought, or uncomfortable situation. Go through this checklist before taking action.

Body-Based Business Method Checklist

1. Nervous System Regulation
    o   Have I used the Nervous System Cheat Sheet to regulate my body?
    o   Am I viewing this through a dysregulated nervous system story? If so, what would a regulated nervous system story look like?
2. Trauma Healing
    o   Have I connected to a sense of Self?
    o   Have I validated my pain and processed my emotions?
    o   Have I dialogued with my parts and identified disempowering beliefs?
    o   Have I anchored into an expanded belief?
    o   Have I expanded my nervous system capacity using the expansion practice?

3. Inspired Action and Protocols
   - o Have I taken inspired action from a regulated state?
   - o Is there a protocol I need to establish to support accessing flow?
   - o Reflection
   - o What have I learned about myself and my business through this experience?
   - o What did I enjoy about using the BBB protocol this time?
   - o What would I do differently next time?
   - o How can I celebrate myself for this experiment?

Protocol 2: Making decisions with emotional and somatic intelligence.

This involves using emotional alchemy and parts work to make balanced, effective, and informed choices under pressure. By following the BBB strategy, you combine creative, logical, and intuitive thinking, giving you access to inspired action and success that might otherwise seem difficult to strategize or plan.

Make decisions when you're mentally and emotionally neutral. If you're more regulated at certain times of the month, use that window to make important decisions.

If you're excited about something, avoid committing immediately. Acknowledge the excitement, and set a rule that you'll wait three days before making a final decision. This gives you time to reflect and ensure that you're acting from a place of clarity.

Establish a protocol for dealing with client requests that trigger strong emotions. Before responding, regulate your nervous system and reflect on the situation to ensure your response aligns with both your boundaries and the client's needs.

Time Management

Time management isn't about managing tasks—it's about leveraging your body's energy and accessing your flow state so that you can bring your full presence and attention to the task at hand.

Protocol 1: Align tasks with energy peaks.

To optimize productivity, focus-intensive tasks should be done when your energy is naturally higher. For instance, if your energy peaks in the morning, use that time to tackle your most challenging tasks. Understand that your energy will fluctuate throughout the month (particularly for women with hormonal cycles) and plan your schedule accordingly.

If you tend to overcommit, use time blocking to create clear, focused work periods and schedule regular breaks. On your calendar, for each task, block out corresponding time so that you can stick to your schedule, achieve your goals, and avoid burnout.

Protocol 2: Make time for breaks and self-care.

If you're someone who often forgets to eat or take breaks, ensure that you schedule them into your day no matter what. This helps maintain your energy and nervous system regulation.

Systems and structure are key to being the leader you need to be. Ensuring that breaks, meals, and self-care are part of your routine is crucial to your long-term success. This means designing your day around your energy levels, integrating both deep work sessions and intentional breaks. For instance, alternate ninety-minute focused work blocks doing the work you tend to procrastinate first, with twenty-minute pauses for something fun and nourishing, like a walk or even a funny video or a call with a friend.

Administrative Management

Administrative management involves the structures, workflows, marketing, sales, and operations that form the backbone of your business. These elements aren't always visible but are critical to the actual functioning of your business.

Protocol 1: Minimize decision-making to reduce anxiety.

Large amounts of decision-making and high-frequency touchpoints can create overwhelm. By reducing daily decision-making through streamlined workflows and delegation, you can preserve mental energy for more important tasks. Here are some ways you could implement this:

- **Batch similar tasks.** Instead of making multiple decisions throughout the day, group similar tasks together. For example, dedicate a block to respond to all emails instead of doing it sporadically, or make decisions about marketing on Tuesdays, instead of making microdecisions throughout the week.
- **Create premade decision trees.** For frequent decisions, like whether to accept a new client or project, design a simple checklist or decision tree.
  o Does this align with my why, my values, and my goals?
  o Do I have the time and resources to take this on without overextending myself?
  o Will it bring long-term value to my business?
- **Delegate.** This one you can always come back to—even if you think you're a pro. There are likely things you're holding onto doing that you just don't need to be.
  o You could use tools or team members to handle recurring tasks. For instance, automate social media posts with a scheduling tool, or have an assistant handle calendar management.

  o Empowering your team members to make more decisions will let you focus your energy on more critical tasks.

Protocol 2: Manage perfectionism and micromanaging.

If you tend to micromanage or want things done a certain way, be aware that this creates a culture of mistrust, both within yourself and with your team. Letting go of control is essential for a regulated nervous system and effective business management.

- Prepare yourself first. Before delegating, regulate your nervous system with tools from pillar 1 or the Nervous System Cheat Sheet. A calm state helps you shift from control to collaboration.
- Delegate clearly. Calm instructions build confidence and increase the likelihood of achieving goals.
  - o Share the goal: "We need a report with insights on X."
  - o Clarify outcomes: "It should cover Y and Z."
  - o Allow creativity: "Use the format you prefer. I'll review once it's ready."
- Regulate when worry creeps in.
  - o If anxiety arises, revisit pillar 1 for tools to regulate and pillar 2 to practice embodying new beliefs about your team's ability to perform, surprise, and support you. Sometimes, it can be helpful to replace "What if it's wrong?" with reminders like "This builds their skills" and "Their approach might surprise me."
- Adopt an attitude of experimentation and reflection. Reflect and learn by answering these questions:
  - o What felt really good about this action?
  - o What didn't feel great?
  - o What would you like to repeat and experience more of?

  o What would you change if you did it again?
- Provide Feedback. I've shared a protocol for this part—see below!

Protocol 3: Create a feedback protocol.

Create a feedback protocol that allows you to engage with your team from a place of curiosity, compassion, and courage, to make sure your business goals are met. We will dive into this a little more below, and while a whole book could be written about how to do this effectively, I'm keeping this short and simple so that you can start using it today.

- Ground yourself. Connect to Self before the conversation, and access feelings of curiosity and compassion. You want to feel like you're on the same team as the person you'll be speaking to—you're both working toward a goal and this conversation is a compassionate, courageous way of figuring out how to get there best.
- Start with connection. Find a way to genuinely connect with them, perhaps complimenting something they did well on the project. The key here is that it must be genuine, not forced. If it's forced, their nervous system will feel it, and it'll feel icky and off for you both.
- Be specific and neutral. Focus on facts, not personal judgments. For example, "The report missed the deadline, which impacted [result]."
- Get curious with open-ended questions. Understand their perspective. Ask them what challenges came up.
- Suggest solutions together. Collaborate on improvements by asking "What can we change to ensure success next time?"
- End with encouragement. Reinforce their capability and offer support: "I'm confident you've got this, and I'm here to help."
- Celebrate yourself and them in a genuine way.

Protocol 4: Use automation effectively.

Automation helps reduce decision-making fatigue by handling repetitive tasks. This frees up mental energy for higher priority tasks and keeps operations running smoothly.

Sales and Marketing

Sales and marketing are some of the most crucial elements in your business but often come with high levels of uncertainty and pressure. Questions like "Where will the next client come from?" or "What if we run out of funding?" can trigger significant stress. Your nervous system can perceive financial uncertainty as a literal threat to survival because money provides both resources and a sense of community.

Protocol 1: Decrease pressure and uncertainty in sales.

Sales and marketing involve a lot of tracking and activity, which can lead to burnout. To reduce this stress, schedule lead generation during low-stress periods, such as when you've just completed a launch, and you're not actively looking to enroll, fundraise or sell—instead you're focusing on nurturing.

Use engagement metrics and feedback from your community to reassure your nervous system that progress is being made. When your body senses demand for your offerings, it will reduce stress, allowing for more creativity and less anxiety.

Protocol 2: Prioritize long-term revenue products for stability.

If financial stability is key to your sense of safety, prioritize long-term revenue streams like retainer-based packages. This creates a consistent income stream and reduces financial pressure.

Understand your team's stress tolerance and set sales targets that keep them motivated and inspired without pushing them into overwhelm.

Protocol 3: Motivation beyond financial support

When financially secure, you might feel less motivated to work. If this is the case, identify what truly drives you—whether it's helping others, building connections, or something else.

Build this motivation into your sales process. For example, if helping others motivates you, reframe sales calls as opportunities for healing and transformation, allowing you to stay engaged without feeling financial pressure.

Protocol 4: Regulate before sales calls.

If you tend to show up to sales calls feeling jittery or anxious, incorporate grounding practices like yoga, breathwork, or even a chat with someone you trust before and after the call.

These grounding practices aren't separate from your sales process—they're an integral part of it. They help you show up to calls feeling grounded and regulated, which enhances your ability to connect with potential clients and close deals.

Relationship Management

Relationship management involves everything related to communication, leadership, conflict resolution, and creating supportive team environments. It's about fostering a sense of connection, trust, and collaboration, where all team members feel secure and valued. Whether you're leading yourself (self-leadership), one employee, or multiple team members, effective leadership is the foundation of business success.

Protocol 1: Lead through strong relationships.

Studies show happy employees who feel safe, respected, and valued and see how their work contributes to a greater goal are more innovative and creative.[23] By focusing on building strong relationships in which trust and joy are deeply ingrained, making working together enjoyable and productive, you'll create a workplace where you, and your team want to consistently show up and take action to see your vision created in the world. You can make this a protocol by taking time at the end of each week, or project to reflect back to each person involved the specific impact their work had on the larger vision and mission.

Protocol 2: Get on the same team.

While we both understand you're literally on the same team, when differences of opinion arise, it's easy for our nervous systems to interpret these differences as threats and start seeing the other person as against you. This activates a stress response, which can lead to avoidance, shut-down, or defensiveness and frustration. This isn't leadership—it's a breakdown in communication.

Instead, the most effective approach is to consistently remind yourself that you're all on the same team, working toward a shared goal. Whenever differences of opinion arise, focus on understanding what's important to the other person.

- Are they protecting their time because they don't believe spending it on one task is worthwhile?

---

23. Konstantinos Papachristopoulos, Marc-Antoine Gradito Dubord, Florence Jauvin, Jacques Forest, and Patrick Coulombe, "Positive Impact, Creativity, and Innovative Behavior at Work: The Mediating Role of Basic Needs Satisfaction" *Behavioral Sciences 13*, no. 12 (2023): 984, https://doi.org/10.3390/bs13120984.

- Are they protecting their reputation because they disagree with your approach to messaging?
- Are they defending their sense of self?

By understanding what's important to the other person, you can affirm their concerns, making them feel seen and secure. Then you can work together to be creative about finding solutions that align with both their needs and the goals of the business.

Protocol 3: Anchor into the qualities of Self.

One of the most effective ways to manage relationships and lead your team is by anchoring into the qualities of your authentic self. When you operate from a place of clarity, compassion, and courage, you're able to communicate effectively, build trust, and foster collaboration. This type of leadership creates an environment where everyone feels valued and motivated to contribute their best work.

That means your job as a leader is to use pillar 2 of the BBB method to manage your own reactions and notice what pulls you out of Self. Perhaps you feel the urge to get things done faster, or maybe you crave more connection yourself. When these internal conflicts come up, it's essential to return to pillar 2. Engage with the parts of yourself that feel resistant, ask them to step aside, and allow your leadership to come from a place of compassion, curiosity, and connection. This approach helps you engage with your team from the qualities of your true self, fostering a work environment built on trust, security, and mutual respect.

Protocol 4: Increase connection through curiosity and active listening.

You can deepen your connection with team members by anchoring yourself in curiosity. Ask yourself two core questions during interactions:

- What is important to this person?
- What makes them feel safe?

By holding these questions in your mind while engaging, you'll notice patterns that help foster trust and security. One way of doing this is to honor the preferences of team members and clients.

During an onboarding process, I noticed an employee preferred working slowly and having plenty of time scheduled for tasks, which made her feel more secure. While I prefer efficiency, I set my preferences aside to ensure she felt at ease by scheduling more than enough time for tasks.

Another team member valued time freedom, so we structured her work to give her as much flexibility as possible. Similarly, one of our clients felt safe and fulfilled when she was productive, so we focused our decision-making around maximizing her productivity.

Protocol 5: Educate your team about the nervous system.

Educate your team about how the nervous system responds to stress and feedback. For example, if you respond with a fight response to feedback, educate your team and yourself on how to manage this. One way to do that might be to take feedback during a walking meeting so that your energy has a place to discharge.

Similarly, if a colleague tends to shut down under stress, mitigate that by changing the feedback environment. They could also try walking when receiving or giving feedback to help discharge energy and keep their nervous system regulated. This keeps everyone out of fight, flight, or freeze states during crucial conversations.

Protocol 6: Respect flow time.

Educating your team on flow state is equally important. Flow state helps everyone feel more effective, get more done, and enjoy their work. You can show your team how entering this focused state not only improves job satisfaction but also helps them reach their goals more efficiently.

Support them by understanding what's important to them and supporting them in developing their own rituals around achieving flow state. Encourage open discussions about what they need to access flow and empower them to create boundaries that protect their productive time.

Similarly, help your team respect your flow time. For example, if you need uninterrupted focus until noon, communicate this boundary clearly, stating you shouldn't be contacted unless there's an emergency. To build trust in this process, you must follow through—if you say you'll be available at noon, then show up at noon.

Respect their flow state as well. If they're deep into focused work, avoid interrupting unless it's truly an emergency. It's important to not create a sense of urgency around nonurgent matters, as this breaks their concentration and can hinder their productivity.

Protocol 7: Manage your relationships with clients carefully.

This involves creating an environment of ease, playfulness, fun, and trust while maintaining professionalism. Below are some examples of different types of clients and how you can use nervous system informed protocols to make these relationships smoother.

The clingy client may require extra support during certain phases of their life. While it can put stress on your nervous system, especially if you feel pressured to respond immediately, I recommend a more nuanced approach rather than avoiding them completely.

- **Set clear boundaries.** Establish clear expectations around communication, such as response times.
- **Stick to your boundaries.** For example, you can have a policy of responding to emails within five days. Stick to that time frame to avoid the urge to constantly check emails, which can create stress.
- **Regulate before responding.** If a client's message triggers anxiety or pressure, take a moment to regulate your nervous system before responding. Only respond at a time that is convenient for you, rather than feeling pressured to answer right away.

At some point in your career, you will encounter a difficult client who constantly pushes boundaries, changes project requirements, or criticizes your work. This can trigger a stress response, pushing you into fight-or-flight mode, which may spiral into shame.

- **Set firm expectations.** Have clear agendas for meetings and set expectations from the beginning.
- **Use emotional awareness.** Manage your emotions by processing them without internalizing the client's behavior.
- **Ground yourself during calls.** Practice deep breathing during calls to stay grounded. Walking before and after calls can help regulate your nervous system, keeping you calm.
- **Don't overextend energy.** Recognize that difficult clients are living in their experience, and you don't have to join them in that space. Stay firm but avoid unnecessary emotional energy.

Sometimes there's a client you love working with so much that you may find yourself relaxing your boundaries or even lowering your rates. Over time, this creates resentment as the client begins taking advantage of those blurred boundaries.

- **Identify your need.** Recognize what need you are getting met by blurring boundaries, whether it's connection, financial security, or enjoyment.
- **Make a conscious decision.** Once you've identified the need, make a conscious decision to either continue the behavior if it serves you or find another way to meet that need. For example, if it's connection you crave, spend more time in your community. If it's financial security, seek another client that can provide that.
- **There's no need for shame.** Neither continuing the relationship nor changing it is wrong. What matters is that you are clear about what you are gaining and choose to move forward with intention.

Protocol 8: Managing your emotions when letting clients go.

At some point, every business will need to let clients go, and this can often be uncomfortable, especially if you have emotional wounds around betrayal or abandonment. Also, if you struggle with endings, this can feel even harder.

- It's essential to process your emotions around the situation, whether disappointment, sadness, grief, or frustration. Understand that these feelings are normal and can be worked through.
- It's important to balance business needs with emotional attachments. Sometimes, letting a client go is necessary for the health of the business—especially if they no longer align with your values or are creating undue stress.

Protocol 9: Managing audience relationships.

Managing audience relationships (e.g., through social media or public communication) involves balancing self-expression with marketing goals while avoiding burnout, and a great place to start is to set boundaries around social media.

- Avoid using it when your body is more sensitive, such as right after waking up or before bed.
- Practice grounding techniques while engaging online to avoid slipping into a passive, hypnotic state.
- Use a timer to limit social media use to twenty-five minutes a day.
- Delegate online interactions to an assistant if possible.

Protocol 10: Navigate your fear of being seen.

Your success is directly correlated to your level of comfort being seen. One way this appears is through content creation. Here are some protocols you can implement so you don't need to confront yourself with that fear in ways that aren't helpful.

- If you feel hesitant to share your thoughts due to insecurities, return to pillar 2 for emotional regulation.
- Do a brain dump before creating content, then sift through it to find what you truly believe.
- Avoid engaging with feedback or analytics—delegate that to an assistant. Let them notify you of anything you need to know.

By following these practices, you'll create more ease and alignment in your relationships, both within your team and with your clients and audience.

EXERCISE: Creating Your Protocols

After going through all the different examples, you should have some ideas and inspiration, so now it's time to begin applying these protocols to your life. I've provided some questions below for you to answer to help you create your own protocols. You can answer them immediately and start implementing your protocols today. However, I also suggest considering these questions throughout the week. Depending on how your brain works best (and this might change at different times in your life) you can do one or both of the options described below.

The first option is to pop the questions into your mind and see what unfolds as you move through your workday and life. You might start noticing small habits, patterns, or approaches you're using that could be tweaked to help you experience more flow and more regulation, so things feel a little less like an uphill battle.

The second option is to pop these questions into a note and put a reminder on your calendar to revisit them once a day or stick a Post-it on your computer (or any place you look at often) so they remain in the forefront of your mind as you move about your day.

Questions to Create Your Own Protocols

Self-Management

What daily rituals or routines could you implement to ground yourself and manage emotional ups and downs before diving into focused work? Consider tools or activities from the Nervous System Cheat Sheet or from what you've learned about your flow state that help your nervous system stay regulated throughout the day.

Admin Management

How can you structure your workday to reduce overwhelm, maintain clarity, and create time for deep, focused work while balancing administrative tasks? What time-management tools or systems would help you stay organized and reduce decision fatigue?

Team Management

What communication protocols can you establish to foster a calm, focused, and collaborative environment within your team? How can you ensure everyone feels supported and able to access flow while still meeting shared objectives?

Sales and Marketing

What parts of your sales and marketing process feel heavy, pressured, or hard? What are ways you could make them feel 10 percent easier, and what structures or automations do you need in place to make that happen?

Relationship Management

What relationships are you spending mental and emotional energy on in a way that is draining? What do you need to let go of these patterns? What boundaries can you establish to protect your energy while maintaining strong, supportive relationships with clients or team members?

Audience Relationships

What boundaries or tools can help you manage social media and audience interactions without burnout? What aspects of relationships to your audience feel easier for you, and how can you do more of that?

As Debbie reflected on these questions, she noticed a profound lack of systems and protocols in her life, as well as a need for deeper, one-on-one support. As far as her lifestyle and business, few things were consistently structured, her IBS was worse than ever, and she was experiencing more aches and pains. She realized that a key part of honoring where she was meant not trying so hard to get rid of her self-doubt, her feelings of being stuck, her desire to hide away from networking opportunities, or her sense of disconnect and questioning.

She had been trying to do everything alone, and she felt like asking for help—really deep help—meant she was failing. She was beginning to see that to achieve her goals she would need more than education, more than awareness, more than practice; she needed a coach and some deeper psychological support, like therapy.

Reflecting on the protocols that would help her take in this support, she set up two main ones:

The first was one-on-one support. Because she knew she needed both therapeutic support and to move her business forward, she reached out to me. We set up a plan for her to receive therapeutic support, as well as coaching with accountability and structure to make sure her business was moving toward its goals.

Then she moved on to structural support. After she scheduled her weekly sessions with me, she blocked out thirty minutes before and after our calls so that she could connect into our calls with a feeling of spaciousness. Then, she identified three repetitive tasks she was doing and delegated them to her assistant. This meant letting go of some control of her schedule and trusting her assistant with more details than usual, but she leaned into that discomfort using the protocols above and was successful.

This decreased her cognitive load (how much energy her brain had to use each day) and freed up more mental energy for her deeper healing work.

Emily felt very balanced reflecting on these questions, happy that she was already naturally maintaining healthy client boundaries, and she decided to refine and strengthen them even further. She implemented a protocol to set clear communication expectations with her clients, establishing a seventy-two-hour response time for inquiries and limiting her responses to the afternoons only. This allowed her to dedicate her mornings to deep, focused work without interruptions—perfect!

Emily also created a client resource guide to teach her clients how to ask for support effectively. This guide outlined how to submit questions and inquiries in a streamlined manner, such as specifying the issue clearly, including necessary details, and using a dedicated submission form. Clients loved the new system, messaging her and her team to say they felt taken care of and that the new guide helped them clarify their thoughts and sometimes even answer their own questions!

With fewer interruptions and clearer communication, Emily had a whole bunch of time and energy on her hands. She picked up a networking event that became a place she felt really seen as herself, less alone in her leadership, and a part of a strong community.

Key Takeaways

- You may notice that lacking systems and protocols can contribute to burnout and physical symptoms. Recognize the importance of psychological support, reduce your expectations when needed, and implement structures that help you manage stress and burnout effectively.

- By incorporating breaks, somatic exercises, and time for reflection into your routine, you can create a sense of balance. Delegating tasks and reviewing progress regularly allows you to stop making constant on-the-fly decisions, giving you more ease and confidence in your leadership.
- With structured leadership and effective delegation, you can foster stronger connections within your team and implement changes that promote equality and inclusivity. Thoughtful leadership combined with the right systems can lead to significant positive outcomes.

Now that you've created protocols that will support you accessing flow state and getting your work out into the world, you're ready to identify and sustain your own definition of success.

Chapter 16

Success

As the year came to a close, it was time to graduate from the Body-Based Business Academy. Debbie, despite the small, occasional steps she managed to take, felt utterly drained, while Emily was thriving, leaving Debbie feeling somewhat jarred. Emily had been invited to speak at a local start-up's gala to share her experience with the Body-Based Business Academy. She had diligently applied all the tools she'd learned, feeling both prepared and confident in her ability to speak publicly—a skill she had worked hard to master. Debbie had also been invited to the gala, though not to speak, and she almost didn't attend. She was tired, in a deep, unshakable way, and didn't think she could muster the energy for such a social occasion. But in the end, she decided to go, unaware that Emily's testimony would change her life.

Both women dressed up for the event, donning their fancy dresses and taking their seats as local press snapped photos and captured the excitement of the evening. About forty-five minutes into the presentation, Debbie was surprised to see Emily walk up to the stage. She hadn't expected Emily to be one of the speakers. But as Emily approached the podium and began to speak, everything started to make sense.

"I started this year feeling anxious, indecisive, and tense," Emily began. "If you had told me back then that I'd be standing here, I wouldn't have believed you. There were definitely moments over the past year that were really difficult and required more courage than I thought I had."

She paused, gathering her thoughts before continuing. "I enrolled in a program designed to support entrepreneurs and leaders like me, one that took a very different approach to business by focusing on the body. It was the Body-Based Business Academy. And to be honest, there were times I wasn't sure if it would work. But I stayed committed, and today, I'm standing here with a deep sense of accomplishment."

Before diving into the details of her achievements, Emily shared a deeper reflection. "Before I talk about the team I've built, the projects I've completed, and the money I've made, I want to share something more important. I've spent this year asking myself what it means to be successful. We often look at leaders who have massive companies, hundreds of employees, or make millions of dollars, and we label them as successful. But for me, success isn't about working harder or doing more. It's not about extracting productivity at the expense of your own well-being. It's about how I feel in my body when I wake up to contribute to the world."

She leaned in, connecting with the audience. "Every day, I ask myself four simple questions: Do I feel good? Do I feel grounded and happy? Am I doing something of value in the world? And will the world be better because of something I did today?"

Emily smiled and continued. "I'm happy to say that for the majority of the past year, I've been able to answer yes to all of those questions. But before I started the Body-Based Business process, I couldn't say that. I was either feeling disconnected or questioning my contribution."

She took a deep breath before sharing more vulnerable insights. "I didn't get here by being perfect. In fact, I've made a lot of mistakes—some that I'm ashamed of and others that I wish I hadn't made. But through this program, I learned to see those mistakes not as failures but as necessary steps forward. Each one gave me more information about what my business, my team, and I needed to grow."

Emily's voice grew more confident. "With this new information, I was able to focus on what to do next, rather than getting stuck in what went wrong. And combining this with actually learning about what my body needs to be resilient—what my nervous system needs to feel supported and regulated—helped me find flow."

She paused again, her tone growing even more passionate. "The truth is, you're never going to figure out what's right for you if you don't learn what your body is communicating to you. You have to know the difference between fear and intuition. When you learn how to tell if loneliness means you should reach out to someone or if it means you should sit with yourself a little longer, you can make choices that serve you. It's about finding that flow, that freedom you feel when you're doing the exact thing you need to do in this world—and protecting that at all costs."

Her gaze swept the audience. "We need more of you. The world needs what you have to offer. You may not get to control everything that happens in your business journey, but you can control how you show up and how much joy and beauty you bring to the world by being yourself, by being lit up, by being healthy. The way you speak to someone creates a ripple effect—it either brings more ease and peace or more harm. And the way you speak to yourself influences how you speak to others. If we want a society where health, support, and ease are available to all of us, we need you to be happy. We need you to do your work. Your vision and your work matter."

Emily's voice softened but remained powerful. "And don't give up. Don't ever give up. No matter how hard things are right now, there's always a next best step. Just because it's hard doesn't mean you've failed. It doesn't mean you've made a mistake—it's just hard right now, and that's okay. This place of discomfort is where your courage grows, where your strength is built."

She finished with a final message of encouragement. "Know that your work matters. Your vision matters. Your way of doing things is enough, and you're going to get there. Allow yourself to be supported—nobody succeeds on their own. There are people, tools, and resources out there waiting to help you. Let them. Keep going. The world needs what you have to offer."

Continue Your Journey

Thank you for sticking with me through the end of this book. I'm truly excited to have you here, and I genuinely believe the world needs your unique contribution. I'd love to support you further on your journey and invite you to share this with the communities that could benefit most.

Here are some additional actions you can take to continue your journey.

- Share the wisdom. If this book resonated with you, share it with a friend or recommend it to someone who could benefit from its insights.
- Stay up-to-date and explore tailored resources. Visit sheridanruth.com to register for email updates containing free tools, podcast episodes, and resources mentioned throughout the book, designed to help you integrate these practices and philosophies into your life and create sustainable changes.
- Join the community. We have a group of amazing individuals who hold similar dreams, desires, and fears along with a commitment to doing good in the world and living from their body and values. You can join us at sheridanruth.com/community.
- Work one-on-one with me. You can probably do this alone—but you don't have to. Personalized guidance helps you see your own blind spots (we all have them), release the pain, tiredness, and

loneliness so many of us entrepreneurs carry, and increase your impact and income. Visit sheridanruth.com/coaching.

Your work matters.

Your vision matters.

Thank you for being here.

With love,

Sher

Acknowledgments

This work is a culmination of many lineages, traditions, and practices that have profoundly influenced me. I wish to honor and thank the wisdom of the yogic and Vedic traditions, depth psychology, Poly Vagal Theory, and Internal Family Systems, all of which have shaped this work. It is also deeply informed by my own journey, through much trial and error, as a lifelong solopreneur.

I am profoundly grateful to the wonderful clients who have trusted me on their journeys and given me the privilege and honor of supporting them. Your courage, growth, and stories have inspired this work in countless ways.

I also want to acknowledge and honor the indigenous lands on which this work was written—the lands of Colombia, Argentina, and Australia. This synthesis is one lens, one perspective, on something humanity has explored and articulated across generations and cultures.

Finally, to the beautiful people in my life who have supported me emotionally and bolstered me with their strength, confidence, and love— thank you. Your presence has been an anchor as I've brought this work to life.

About the Author

Sheridan Ruth is a Nervous System Specialist who has guided hundreds of clients spanning multiple continents and industries through thousands of coaching hours. Her clients consistently report a decrease in burnout symptoms, breakthroughs in confidence, income, and alignment with their purpose, creating ripple effects in their communities and industries. An expert in Community Development, Sustainability, Yoga Psychology, Ayurveda, and Integrative Somatic Trauma Therapy, Sheridan has used her extensive knowledge and personal experience to create a unique coaching model called Body Based Business™ to teach clients how to build sustainable, profitable, and purposeful businesses using the wisdom of their nervous system. She believes each individual has immense power to create positive cultural change, and her goal is to help them do so with more ease, efficiency, resilience, innovation, and creativity.

When not helping her clients change the world, Sheridan works as a Committee Member for the Australia Alopecia Areata Foundation, helping bring awareness to Alopecia Universalis, an incurable autoimmune disease that results in total hair loss.

Sheridan lives in Melbourne, Australia, where she loves to eat cheese, drink wine, swim in rivers, and dance.

You can find more about Sheridan and Body Based Business™ at sheridanruth.com.

www.ingramcontent.com/pod-product-compliance
Lightning Source LLC
Chambersburg PA
CBHW071718120626
46550CB00001B/284